Hacking The LSAT

LSAT Preptest 71 Explanations

A Study Guide for LSAT 71
(Includes Logic Games Diagrams)

Graeme Blake

ISBN 13: 978-1-927997-01-7
ISBN 10: 1-927997-01-1

Testimonials

Self-study is my preferred way to prep, but I often felt myself missing a few questions each test. Especially for Logic Games, I wanted to see those key inferences which I just couldn't seem to spot on my own. That's where *Hacking The LSAT* came in. These solutions have been a tremendous help for my prep, and in training myself to think the way an experienced test taker would.

- Spencer B.

Graeme paraphrases the question in plain terms, and walks through each step in obtaining the right answer in a very logical way. This book uses the same techniques as other guides, but its so much more consistent and concise! By the time you read through all the tests, you've gradually developed your eye for the questions. Using this book is a great way to test your mastery of techniques!

- Sara L.

Graeme's explanations have the most logical and understandable layout I've seen in an LSAT prep book. The explanations are straightforward and easy to understand, to the point where they make you smack your forehead and say 'of course!

- Michelle V.

"Graeme is someone who clearly demonstrates not only LSAT mastery, but the ability to explain it in a compelling manner. This book is an excellent addition to whatever arsenal you're amassing to tackle the LSAT."

- J.Y. Ping, 7Sage LSAT,
www.7Sage.com

I did not go through every single answer but rather used the explanations to see if they could explain why my answer was wrong and the other correct. I thought the breakdown of "Type", "Conclusion", "Reasoning" and "Analysis" was extremely useful in simplifying the question. As for quality of the explanations I'd give them a 10 out of 10.

- Christian F.

LSAT PrepTests come with answer keys, but it isn't sufficient to know whether or not you picked the credited choice to any given question. The key to making significant gains on this test is understanding the logic underlying the questions.

This is where Graeme's explanations really shine. You may wonder whether your reasoning for a specific question is sound. For the particularly challenging questions, you may be at a complete loss as to how they should be approached.

Having these questions explained by Graeme who scored a 177 on the test is akin to hiring an elite tutor at a fraction of the price. These straightforward explanations will help you improve your performance and, more fundamentally, enhance your overall grasp of the test content.

- Morley Tatro, Cambridge LSAT,
www.cambridgelsat.com

Through his conversational tone, helpful introductions, and general recommendations and tips, Graeme Blake has created an enormously helpful companion volume to *The Next Ten Actual Official LSATs*. He strikes a nice balance between providing the clarity and basic explanation of the questions that is needed for a beginner and describing the more complicated techniques that are necessary for a more advanced student.

Even though the subject matter can be quite dry, Graeme succeeds in making his explanations fun and lighthearted. This is crucial: studying for the LSAT is a daunting and arduous task. By injecting some humor and keeping a casual tone, the painful process of mastering the LSAT becomes a little less painful.

When you use *Hacking The LSAT* in your studying, you will feel like you have a fun and knowledgeable tutor guiding you along the way.

- Law Schuelke, LSAT Tutor,
www.lawLSAT.com

Graeme's explanations are clear, concise and extremely helpful. They've seriously helped me increase my understanding of the LSAT material!

- Jason H.

Graeme's book brings a different view to demystifying the LSAT. The book not only explains the right and wrong answers, but teaches you how to read the reading comprehension and the logical reasoning questions. His technique to set up the games rule by rule help me not making any fatal mistakes in the set up. The strategies he teaches can be useful for someone starting as much as for someone wanting to perfect his strategies. Without his help my LSAT score would have been average, he brought my understanding of the LSAT and my score to a higher level even if english is not my mother tongue.

- Patrick Du.

This book is a must buy for any who are looking to pass or improve their LSAT, I highly recommend it.

- Patrick Da.

This book was really useful to help me understand the questions that I had more difficulty on. When I was not sure as to why the answer to a certain question was that one, the explanations helped me understand where and why I missed the right answer in the first place. I recommend this book to anyone who would like to better understand the mistakes they make.

- Pamela G.

Graeme's book is filled with thoughtful and helpful suggestions on how to strategize for the LSAT test. It is well-organized and provides concise explanations and is definitely a good companion for LSAT preparation.

- Lydia L.

The explanations are amazing, great job. I can hear your voice in my head as I read through the text.

- Shawn M.

Hacking the LSAT, especially the logic games sections, was extremely helpful to my LSAT preparation.

The one downside to self study is that sometimes we do not know why we got a question wrong and thus find it hard to move forward. Graeme's book fixes that; it offers explanations and allows you to see where you went wrong. This is an extremely helpful tool and I'd recommend it to anybody that's looking for an additional study supplement.

- Joseph C.

Regardless of how well you're scoring on the LSAT, this book is very helpful. I used it for LR and RC. It breaks down and analyzes each question without the distraction of classification and complicated methods you'll find in some strategy books. Instead of using step-by-step procedures for each question, the analyses focus on using basic critical thinking skills and common sense that point your intuition in the right direction. Even for questions you're getting right, it still helps reinforce the correct thought process. A must-have companion for reviewing prep tests.

- Christine Y.

Take a thorough mastery of the test, an easygoing demeanor, and a genuine desire to help, and you've got a solid resource for fine-tuning your approach when you're tirelessly plowing through test after test. Written from the perspective of a test-taker, this book should help guide your entire thought process for each question, start to finish.

- Yoni Stratievsky, Harvard Ready, www.harvardready.com

This LSAT guide is the best tool I could have when preparing for the LSAT. Not only does Graeme do a great job of explaining the sections as a whole, he also offers brilliant explanations for each question. He takes the time to explain why an answer is wrong, which is far more helpful when trying to form a studying pattern.

- Amelia F.

LSAT 71 Explanations
Table Of Contents

Introduction

The LSAT is a hard test.

The only people who write the LSAT are smart people who did well in University. The LSAT takes the very best students, and forces them to compete.

If the test's difficulty shocked you, this is why. The LSAT is a test designed to be hard for smart people.

That's the bad news. But there's hope. The LSAT is a *standardized* test. It has patterns. It can be learned.

To get better, you have to review your mistakes. Many students write tests and move on, without fully understanding their mistakes.

This is understandable. The LSAC doesn't publish official explanations for most tests. It's hard to be sure why you were wrong.

That's where this book comes in. It's a companion for LSAT 71, the December 2013 LSAT.

This book lets you see where you went wrong. It has a full walk through of each question and of every answer choice. You can use this book to fix your mistakes, and make sure you understand *everything*.

By getting this book, you've shown that you're serious about beating this test. I sincerely hope it helps you get the score you want.

There are a few things that I'd like to highlight.

Logical Reasoning: It can be hard to identify conclusions in LR. You don't get feedback on whether you identified the conclusion correctly.

This book gives you that feedback. I've identified the conclusion and the reasoning for each argument. Try to find these on your own beforehand, and make sure they match mine.

Logic Games: Do the game on your own before looking at my explanation. You can't think about a game unless you're familiar with the rules. Once you read my explanations, draw my diagrams yourself on a sheet of paper. You'll understand them much better by recopying them.

Reading Comprehension: You should form a mental map of the passage. This helps you locate details quickly. Make a 1-2 line summary of each paragraph (it can be a mental summary).

I've written my own summaries for each passage. They show the minimum amount of information that you should know after reading a passage, without looking back.

I've included line references in my explanations. You do not need to check these each time. They're only there in case you aren't sure where something is.

Do these three things, and you can answer most Reading Comprehension questions with ease.:

1. Know the point of the passage.
2. Understand the passage, in broad terms. Reread anything you don't understand.
3. Know where to find details. That's the point of the paragraph summaries. I usually do mine in my head, and they're shorter than what I've written.

Review This Book

Before we start, I'd like to ask you a favor. I'm an independent LSAT instructor. I don't have a marketing budget.

But I do my best to make good guides to the LSAT. If you agree, I would love it if you took two minutes to write a review on amazon.com

People judge a book by its reviews. So if you like this guide you can help others discover it. I'd be very grateful.

Good luck!

Graeme

p.s. I'm a real person, and I want to know how the LSAT goes and what you think of this book. Send me an email at graeme@lsathacks.com!

p.p.s. For more books, check out the further reading section at the back. I'm also offering a free half hour LSAT lesson if you fill out a survey.

How To Use This Book

The word "Hacking" in the title is meant in the sense used by the tech world and Lifehacker: "solving a problem" or "finding a better way".

The LSAT can be beaten, but you need a good method. My goal is for you to use this book to understand your mistakes and master the LSAT.

This book is *not* a replacement for practicing LSAT questions on your own.

You have to try the questions by yourself first. When you review, try to see why you were wrong *before* you look at my explanations.

Active review will teach you to fix your own mistakes. The explanations are there for when you have difficulty solving on a question on your own or when you want another perspective on a question.

When you *do* use the explanations, have the question on hand. These explanations are not meant to be read alone. You should use them to help you think about the questions more deeply.

Most of the logical reasoning explanations are pretty straightforward. Necessary assumption questions are often an exception, so I want to give you some guidance to help you interpret the explanations.

The easiest way to test the right answer on a necessary assumption question is to "negate" it.

You negate a statement by making it false, in the slightest possible way. For example, the negation of "The Yankees will win all their games" is "The Yankees will *not* win all their games (they will lose at least one)."

You *don't* have to say that the Yankees will lose *every* game. That goes too far.

If the negation of an answer choice proves the conclusion wrong, then that answer is *necessary* to the argument, and it's the correct answer.

Often, I negate the answer choices when explaining necessary assumption questions, so just keep in mind why they're negated.

Logic games also deserve special mention.

Diagramming is a special symbolic language that you have to get comfortable with to succeed.

If you just *look* at my diagrams without making them yourself, you may find it hard to follow along. You can only learn a language by using it yourself.

So you will learn *much* more if you draw the diagrams on your own. Once you've seen how I do a setup, try to do it again by yourself.

With constant practice, you *will* get better at diagramming, and soon it will come naturally.

But you must try on your own. Draw the diagrams.

Note that when you draw your own diagrams, you don't have to copy every detail from mine. For example, I often leave off the numbers when I do linear games. I've included them in the book, because they make it easier for you to follow along.

But under timed conditions, I leave out many details so that I can draw diagrams faster. If you practice making drawings with fewer details, they become just as easy to understand.

Keep diagrams as minimal as possible.

If you simply don't *like* the way I draw a certain rule type, then you can substitute in your own style of diagram. Lots of people succeed using different styles of drawing.

Just make sure your replacement is easy to draw consistently, and that the logical effect is the same. I've chosen these diagrams because they are clear, they're easy to draw, and they *keep you from forgetting rules*.

I've included line references to justify Reading Comprehension Answers. Use these only in case you're unsure about an explanation. You don't have to go back to the passage for every line reference.

Short Guide to Logical Reasoning

LR Question Types

Must be True: The correct answer is true.

Most Strongly Supported: The correct answer is probably true.

Strengthen/Weaken: The answer is correct if it even slightly strengthens/weakens the argument.

Parallel Reasoning: The correct answer will mirror the argument's structure exactly. It is often useful to diagram these questions (but not always).

Sufficient Assumption: The correct answer will prove the conclusion. It's often useful to diagram sufficient assumption questions. For example:

The conclusion is: A → D

There is a gap between premises and conclusion:

A   B → C → D   **missing link:** A → B or B̶ → A̶

A → B → C   D   **missing link:** C → D or D̶ → C̶

A → B   C → D   **missing link:** B → C or C̶ → B̶

The right answer will provide the missing link.

Necessary Assumption: The correct answer will be essential to the argument's conclusion. Use the negation technique: If the correct answer is false (negated), then the argument falls apart.
The negation of hot is "not hot" rather than cold.

Point at Issue: Point at Issue questions require two things. **1.** The two speakers must express an opinion on something. **2.** They must disagree about it.

Flawed Reasoning: The correct answer will be a description of a reasoning error made in the argument. It will often be worded very abstractly.

Practice understanding the answers, right and wrong. Flawed Reasoning answers are very abstract, but they all mean something. Think of examples to make them concrete and easier to understand.

Basic Logic

Take the phrase: "All cats have tails."

"Cats" is the sufficient condition. Knowing that something is a cat is "sufficient" for us to say that it has a tail. "Tails" is a necessary condition, because you can't be a cat without a tail. You can draw this sentence as C → T

The **contrapositive** is a correct logical deduction, and reads "anything without a tail is not a cat." You can draw this as T̶ → C̶. Notice that the terms are reversed, and negated.

Incorrect Reversal: "Anything with a tail is a cat." This is a common logical error on the LSAT.

T → C   (Wrong! Dogs have tails and aren't cats.)

Incorrect Negation: "If it is not a cat, it doesn't have a tail." This is another common error.

C̶ → T̶ (Wrong! Dogs aren't cats, but have tails.)

General Advice: Always remember what you are looking for on each question. The correct answer on a strengthen question would be incorrect on a weaken question.

Watch out for subtle shifts in emphasis between the stimulus and the incorrect answer choices. An example would be the difference between "how things are" and "how things should be."

Justify your answers. If you're tempted to choose an answer choice that says something like the sentence below, then be sure you can fill in the blank:

Answer Choice Says: "The politician attacked his opponents' characters",

Fill In The Blank: "The politician said _____ about his opponents' characters."

If you cannot say what the attack was, you can't pick that answer. This applies to many things. You must be able to show that the stimulus supports your idea.

A Few Logic Games Tips

Rule 1: When following along with my explanations....draw the diagrams yourself, too!

This book will be much more useful if you try the games by yourself first. You must think through games on your own, and no book will do that for you. You must have your mind in a game to solve it.

Use the explanations when you find a game you can't understand on your own, or when you want to know how to solve a game more efficiently.

Some of the solutions may seem impossible to get on your own. It's a matter of practice. When you learn how to solve one game efficiently, solving other games becomes easier too.

Try to do the following when you solve games:

Work With What Is Definite: Focus on what must be true. Don't figure out every possibility.

Draw Your Deductions: Unsuccessful students often make the same deductions as successful students. But the unsuccessful students forget their deductions, 15 seconds later! I watch this happen.

Draw your deductions, or you'll forget them. Don't be arrogant and think this doesn't happen to you. It would happen to *me* if I didn't draw my deductions.

Draw Clear Diagrams: Many students waste time looking back and forth between confusing pictures. They've done everything right, but can't figure out their own drawings!

You should be able to figure out your drawings 3 weeks later. If you can't, then they aren't clear enough. I'm serious: look back at your old drawings. Can you understand them? If not, you need a more consistent, cleaner system.

Draw Local Rules: When a question gives you a new rule (a local rule), draw it. Then look for deductions by combining the new rule with your existing rules. Then double-check what you're being asked and see if your deduction is the right answer. This works 90% of the time for local rule questions. And it's fast.

If you don't think you have time to draw diagrams for each question, practice drawing them faster. It's a learnable skill, and it pays off.

Try To Eliminate a Few Easy Answer Choices First: You'll see examples in the explanations that show how certain deductions will quickly get rid of 1-3 answer choices on many questions. This saves time for harder answer choices and it frees up mental space.

You don't have to try the answer choices in order, without thinking about them first.

Split Games Into Two Scenarios When Appropriate: If a rule only allows something to be one of two ways (e.g. F is in 1 or 7), then draw two diagrams: one with F in 1, and one with F in 7. This leads to extra deductions surprisingly often. And it always makes the game easier to visualize.

Combine Rules To Make Deductions: Look for variables that appear in multiple rules. These can often be combined. Sometimes there are no deductions, but it's a crime not to look for them.

Reread The Rules: Once you've made your diagram, reread the rules. This lets you catch any mistakes, which are fatal. It doesn't take very long, and it helps you get more familiar with the rules.

Draw Rules Directly On The Diagram: Mental space is limited. Three rules are much harder to remember than two. When possible, draw rules on the diagram so you don't have to remember them.

Memorize Your Rules: You should memorize every rule you can't draw on the diagram. It doesn't take long, you'll go faster, and you'll make fewer mistakes. Try it, it's not that hard.

If you spend 30 seconds doing this, you'll often save a minute by going through the game faster.

You should also make a numbered list of rules that aren't on the diagram, in case you need to check them.

Section I - Logical Reasoning

Question 1

QUESTION TYPE: Sufficient Assumption

CONCLUSION: The agency is unlikely to achieve its goal.

REASONING: The agency is selling the banks. The banking system will not be strengthened if the former owners buy them back.

ANALYSIS: Most of this argument is fluff. The argument starts after the word "but": the banking system will be weaker if the former owners buy their banks back. Pay attention to words like "but", they show the author's opinion and evidence.

So we know exactly one reason that the plan could fail: the former owners buy back the banks. You can put this into a conditional statement:

Buy Back --> Fail

To prove that the plan will fail, we just need to show that the sufficient condition will happen.

A. The stimulus doesn't mention whether all the banks must be sold. Maybe the plan can succeed even if some banks don't find buyers.
B. The stimulus doesn't say it's a problem for one owner to buy multiple banks. Maybe there are thousands of banks for sale. It surely wouldn't be a problem if one owner bought two small banks.
C. This answer aims to trap you because you assumed that the no one will buy banks unless the economy is stronger. The argument didn't mention the economy. We have no idea how the economy relates to the banking system.
D. The banks sold by the agency *failed*. The government had to buy take them over. The country's other banks *didn't* fail, so presumably they will be stronger. It's reasonable that the failed banks will be weaker for some time.
E. CORRECT. This shows there are two possibilities: either the banks won't sell, or the owners will buy them back. Either option means the plan failed.

Question 2

QUESTION TYPE: Method of Reasoning

CONCLUSION: Falling circulation and falling advertising are the real reasons newspapers are in trouble.

REASONING: The inflation adjusted price of newsprint is no higher than it was ten years ago.

ANALYSIS: The newspapers said newsprint prices are the cause of their troubles. The author destroys this argument by showing that newsprint is not more expensive than it used to be. The author proposes an alternate cause: falling circulation and advertising.

Note that this alternate cause is not well supported. The author hasn't proven these factors are hurting newspapers. But we only need to analyze the structure of the argument: the author disproves a claim, and proposes a rival claim.

Three wrong answers mention criticism of a practice or method. The argument doesn't mention or criticize any methods. An example of such criticism would be "The newspaper industry uses ink, but this is costly. They should use laser printers."

A. What popular analogy? An analogy is a comparison between two similar situations. That doesn't happen here. If you chose this answer you should look at the Wikipedia article on analogies; the LSAT mentions them frequently.
B. It's true that this argument uses historical data. But not to raise doubts about the effectiveness of an approach. The argument merely uses historical data to disprove a point in an argument.
C. Similar to B. The argument doesn't mention any methods or criticize any methods.
D. CORRECT. The explanation is newsprint. The argument challenges this and introduces another explanation: advertising and circulation.
E. Same as B and C. The argument doesn't criticize any practices.

10

Question 3

QUESTION TYPE: Flawed Reasoning

CONCLUSION: Alcohol consumption does more good than harm.

REASONING: Moderate alcohol consumption has a few good effects.

ANALYSIS: There are two flaws with this argument.

1. The author uses evidence about "moderate" alcohol consumption, then makes a conclusion about all alcohol consumption. Watch for concept shifts.
2. The author gives evidence of alcohol's positive effects, and doesn't mention negative effects. The author then makes a conclusion about the *net* effects of alcohol. You always have to consider both benefit and harm.

This question shows that you have to be careful when you pre-phrase answers. The right answer uses the first flaw. If you only spotted the second flaw and fixated on it, you could easily miss the right answer on this otherwise easy question.

Whenever I form a pre-phrase, I am ready to abandon it if I don't see it in the answers.

_____

A. The argument doesn't mention why people chose to drink alcohol. The argument is about alcohol's effects, not how people use it.
B. The argument doesn't mention popular belief. This answer is completely unsupported.
C. This isn't a flaw. I can truthfully say that "pens can be used to write". It doesn't matter that pencils can also be used to write, my first statement is still true. So alcohol can be beneficial even if other things are also beneficial.
D. **CORRECT.** The conclusion is about *all* alcohol consumption, including binge drinking. The evidence is only about moderate consumption.
E. Alcohol doesn't have to harm *all* bacteria. Alcohol would potentially be useful even if it killed only some types of harmful bacteria.

Question 4

QUESTION TYPE: Complete the Argument

CONCLUSION: Grodex Corporation should use the innovative new educational methods.

REASONING: Grodex Corporation generally requires creative workers. Childhood education shows that innovative methods produce creativity while traditional methods produce memorization.

ANALYSIS: You always have to watch for shifts in concepts. All of the educational evidence in the argument is about *children*. And you know from real life that children are different from adults.

The argument ends on "because". So we are not looking for a conclusion. We are looking for a reason for the conclusion.

To prove that the innovative methods will work for Grodex, we need to show that the methods that work with children will also work well with adults.

_____

A. Nonsense. The argument doesn't even mention high school. If you chose this, you need to focus more directly on what's said in the stimulus.
B. The argument wasn't making a comparison of using educational seminars vs. not using them. Instead, the argument was about what *type* of educational seminars to use.
C. This tells us the seminars might not be effective. It doesn't tell us what type of seminar to use.
D. **CORRECT.** This shows that the evidence about children is also applicable to the adults who will take Grodex's seminars.
E. The argument doesn't say whether creativity and memorization are linked. It's not clear how this proposed linkage is relevant to adult educational seminars. If the two were linked, would that change Grodex's actions?

Question 5

QUESTION TYPE: Identify The Conclusion

CONCLUSION: Colonizing other planets would only be a temporary solution to overcrowding.

REASONING: Earth will be too crowded if our population keeps growing at a geometric rate. Even if we send half the population to Mars, population growth will soon leave Earth just as crowded.

ANALYSIS: LSAT authors usually use the phrase "some say" to indicate an opinion they will disagree with. This argument does that in the second sentence. Then this author says "however" in the third sentence to indicate that they do disagree with the opinion in the second sentence. That's the conclusion.

Note that the author's conclusion is about what would be true *IF* the population keeps growing geometrically. The author doesn't say that the population *WILL* keep growing geometrically. This is an important distinction on the LSAT, and it eliminates two answers.

A. This first sentence is not the conclusion. It is just a fact that supports the conclusion and adds context to the argument. .
B. The author didn't say population *will* continue to grow geometrically. She just said what would happen *if* population grew geometrically.
C. This is just a fact that supports the author's point. Since this is true, then it's likely that in a few centuries we will have one person per square foot *if* population grows geometrically.
D. Same as B. The author didn't say that population *will* grow geometrically.
E. **CORRECT.** The word "however" in the third sentence indicates that the third sentence is the conclusion. The author disagrees with the opinion in the second sentence. Whenever an LSAT author says "some say", then their conclusion is probably disagreement with the "some say" opinion.

Question 6

QUESTION TYPE: Strengthen

CONCLUSION: The complexity of chocolate probably masks the low fat flavor.

REASONING: Studies compared regular and low fat versions of ice cream flavors. Compared to regular ice cream, people dislike low fat vanilla, but they don't mind low fat chocolate. Chocolate has a very complex flavor.

ANALYSIS: This argument makes a classic LSAT error. The author makes a comparison between chocolate and vanilla, but they don't give us any information about vanilla! A comparison must give information about both groups.

So, we don't know anything about vanilla. Maybe it's complex too! In that case, we'd need another explanation for low-fat chocolate's appeal.

A. It doesn't matter whether people prefer chocolate to vanilla. The argument's comparison is between full fat and low fat versions of the *same* flavors.
B. If you picked this, you probably assumed that an experiment shouldn't be biased. But in this case, the bias would be equally present in both the chocolate and vanilla experiments. Yet the two experiments had different results. So knowledge of the fat content couldn't have caused the difference between chocolate and vanilla.
C. The argument didn't say chocolate worked because people *liked* it. The argument proposed that the complexity of chocolate's compounds *masked* the low fat flavor.
D. **CORRECT.** The author made a comparison between chocolate and vanilla, but didn't tell us anything about vanilla! This answer completes the comparison: chocolate is indeed more complex. Therefore complexity could have caused the difference.
E. Awareness isn't relevant. People *perceive* the complexity of chocolate when they eat it, whether or not they are *aware* chocolate is complex. Also note that this answer doesn't say the people *in the studies* were aware of complexity – it only says "most people" are aware of complexity.

Question 7

QUESTION TYPE: Identify The Conclusion

CONCLUSION: Gillette's argument isn't convincing.

REASONING: Gillette pointed out some benefits to knowing genetics. But Gillette ignores the fact that knowledge of the human genome might be harmful.

ANALYSIS: On "identify the conclusion" questions, you don't need to consider whether the argument is good or bad. You just need to identify what the author is saying.

The author thinks Gillette is wrong. The "however, because" indicates this conclusion. What comes before the "however" is the conclusion, and what comes after "because" is the evidence.

Note that the ethicist has not said whether she thinks genetic research is a *bad* idea. She's merely pointing out that Gillette's argument is unconvincing. You can disagree with an argument without believing in the opposite conclusion.

A. The ethicist didn't even say this. She may agree with Gillette that knowledge of the genetic code will cure genetic disorders.
B. The fact in this answer is just evidence. The author says this knowledge is something Gillette fails to consider, and Gillette is not persuasive *because* he fails to consider it.
C. The ethicist did not say whether we shouldn't pursue genetic research. She just said Gillette's conclusion is not supported.
The ethicist thinks there is an *absence of evidence* that genetic research is good. But that doesn't mean she thinks there is definitive evidence that it is a bad thing. She may simply be undecided on its benefits.
D. Same as A. The ethicist didn't say Gillette is wrong about genetic disorders. Maybe mapping the genome will prevent 3,000 disorders, but harm us in other ways.
E. **CORRECT.** The "however, because" indicates this is the conclusion. If "however" is in the middle of a sentence, then whatever comes before the however is usually the conclusion.

Question 8

QUESTION TYPE: Most Strongly Supported

FACTS:
1. Subjects listened to music.
2. Under hypnosis, half were asked to remember the music.
3. Under hypnosis, the other half were asked to remember the movie they watched.
4. Both groups gave equally confident and detailed descriptions.

ANALYSIS: Both groups were under hypnosis, and listened to music. One group was told they heard music, the other was told they saw a movie. The second group remembered seeing a movie.

So we've got an experiment with two groups, and *one* difference between them: one group was told a lie, and they believed it.

We can't conclude that hypnosis alone is the cause of anything. *Both* groups were under hypnosis, and the first group behaved normally. All we can say is that the lie was influential while under hypnosis.

As a side note, "equally confident" could mean that both groups were equally *unconfident*.

A. The stimulus didn't give us information to evaluate most claims made about hypnosis.
B. The stimulus only told us about one situation where hypnosis hurt recall. That's not enough information. Maybe in other circumstances hypnosis can improve recall.
C. Way too strong. We know in *one* situation hypnosis led to false memories. But maybe hypnosis doesn't mislead in most situations.
D. **CORRECT** The second group remembered a movie they hadn't seen. Based on common sense, telling them that they saw a movie must have caused this. People would normally know they hadn't seen a movie.
E. In the stimulus, the movie group was given *false* visual memories: this isn't an enhancement.

13

Question 9

QUESTION TYPE: Method of Reasoning

CONCLUSION: A baby's health depends on how much food the mother gets while she is pregnant.

REASONING: There was a correlation between babies' birth weights and the success of crops the year before.

ANALYSIS: This argument has two flaws. First, it uses evidence from a correlation to prove causation. This never works. Second, it switches terms inappropriately. Stop – before reading this explanation, look at the reasoning and conclusion again – try to spot the shifts in terms.

Did you find it? The argument switches from birth weight to health and from crop success to food access. These shifts aren't warranted. First, birth weights. A higher birth weight doesn't necessarily mean a baby is healthier. The argument should have made this explicit.

Second, crop success. Maybe crop success doesn't lead to more food for mothers. This could be a region of farmers. When crops succeed, the mothers are richer, less stressed, etc. But perhaps they normally have enough food either way.

A. CORRECT. See the explanation above. The "claimed correlation" is between birth weights and crops. The causal relation is between health and food access.

B. An example of this would be "....therefore, babies' birth weights are *only* affected by crop success". The argument didn't say anything like that.

C. An example of this would be "....since there used to be a correlation between crops and birth weights, there is still such a correlation."

D. An example of this would be "....because birth weights and crop records are linked, there must be a common cause. Maybe weather explains both crop success and heavier birth weights."

E. There are two reasons this is wrong. First, the argument didn't *explain* any causal relations. Second, there *aren't* two causal relations! The relation between crop success and birth weights is just a correlation.

Question 10

QUESTION TYPE: Point at Issue

ARGUMENTS: Vincent says that science requires measurement, and happiness can't be measured because it is entirely subjective.

Yolanda points out that optometry relies on subjective reports, and optometry is scientific. Yolanda is implying that subjective reports can be used to measure things.

ANALYSIS: For point at issue questions, you must pick something that both debaters explicitly disagree about. You need the two debaters to answer a firm "yes" and "no" to the answer. So each answer must meet two criteria:

1. Both debaters have a clear opinion on the answer.
2. If you asked the debaters whether they agreed with the answer, one would answer "yes" and the other would answer "no".

This lets you eliminate some answers quickly. For instance, Vincent doesn't mention optometry. We can't know his opinion on it, so any answer that mentions optometry is out.

A. Yolanda doesn't say whether she thinks happiness is entirely subjective.

B. Vincent might agree optometry is subjective. Perhaps he thinks optometry has a non-subjective component that Yolanda is ignoring.

C. CORRECT. Yolanda says optometry is scientific, and relies on objective reports. Vincent says that science requires measurement, and that subjectivity must be measured.

D. Yolanda doesn't say whether happiness research is *as* scientific as optometry. Her argument is just that happiness can be scientific, despite its subjectivity. So we don't know what Yolanda thinks. Vincent has no opinion on this question.

E. This answer just gets Richard's belief backwards. He believed "Subjective --> ~~Measured~~". This answer says "~~Measured~~ --> Subjective". So neither author believes this answer.

Question 11

QUESTION TYPE: Role in Argument

CONCLUSION: Increasing population in cities may decrease nationwide pollution.

REASONING: City dwellers use mass transport and live in more efficient homes. Thus, people in cities produce less pollution per capita.

ANALYSIS: To find the conclusion, ask yourself "what are they trying to tell me?". Everything in this argument supports the claim that moving people to cities will reduce pollution.

Conclusion words are useful, but can be misleading. The final sentence uses the word "thus". The final sentence is *a* conclusion, but it's an intermediate conclusion. The fact that city dwellers produce less pollution per capita supports the first sentence: we might decrease pollution by moving people to cities.

Note that the first sentence also has conclusion indicators. "Although....may" indicates the author's opinion, which is usually the conclusion.

———————————

A. The LSAT draws a line between what should be and what is. This question only talks about what is. This answer talks about what "should" happen. We don't know whether people *should* move to cities. Pollution is not the only factor.
B. Reread the argument carefully. It did *not* say that cities aren't polluted. NYC is definitely more polluted than Maine. But, *per capita,* the people in cities produce less pollution.
C. The first sentence is not useless fluff. Notice that it says "although....may actually". Those words indicate the first sentence is the author's opinion, and therefore a conclusion.
D. The first sentence starts with "although". That word indicates that the second part of a sentence will be *in contrast* to the first part.
E. **CORRECT.** Ask yourself "why is the author telling us this?" Everything supports the first sentence. The words "although....may actually" indicate that the first sentence is the author's opinion. The rest of the argument supports this opinion.

Question 12

QUESTION TYPE: Strengthen

CONCLUSION: The mountain snowpack in the Rockies will probably melt earlier, which will cause greater floods and less water for summer.

REASONING: Global warming will probably increase winter temperatures in the Rockies. This will cause more precipitation to fall as rain rather than snow.

ANALYSIS: This is actually a pretty good argument. Why does it need strengthening? Because the conclusion is probabilistic. Further evidence will help prove the probability correct.

As for why the argument is pretty good, it has to do with the relevant authority of the climatologist. I've written a note on the next page about this. You do *not* need to know about the note to get 175+, but you may find the information interesting nonetheless.

———————————

A. The argument said *rain* will cause flooding. This answer says there will be more precipitation, but that could be snow. Global warming has led to more snow in some regions.
B. **CORRECT.** The situation in this answer matches the stimulus exactly. So it strengthens the conclusion. The cause is leading to the effect in other mountain regions, so we can expect the same to be true in the Rockies.
C. This could be true, but how does it strengthen the argument? The argument was talking about the entire Rocky Mountain region, and the effect global warming would have.
   This answer talks about specific, milder regions within the Rockies. That doesn't necessarily tell us what global warming will do. Those mild regions have had thousands of years to adapt, while global warming is happening very fast.
D. This isn't even talking about mountains. Irrelevant. Mountain regions could diverge completely from the average.
E. The stimulus didn't talk about larger snowpacks. Global warming makes snowpacks melt faster, but they may not be larger.

Note on Relevant Authority (Q12)

The speaker is a "climatologist" instead of a "politician" or an "environmentalist". The LSAT has previously used relevant expertise to allow an author to speak from authority. The issue isn't strictly relevant to answering this question, but make sure you note who's speaking on LR questions.

This is a strengthen question, which usually indicates a flawed argument. But given the authority of the speaker, this may actually be a good argument. The fact that the speaker is a climatologist certainly makes the argument more compelling than it otherwise would be. We can assume a climatologist has relevant expertise and is correct when they say that winter temperatures will rise in the rockies, and that more precipitation will fall as rain.

We can also believe the speaker when they say this means that the mountain snowpack will probably melt earlier, and cause flooding, etc. So why does this argument need strengthening at all? Because it says "probably". Probably is a weak statement – it indicates the climatologist isn't certain in their conclusion. Supporting evidence is *always* useful for a probabilistic conclusion, no matter the authority of the speaker.

A second anecdote to demonstrate that the identity of a speaker can be relevant: I once challenged question 25, section 3 of LSAT Preptest 64. I received a thorough reply, which included this quote "In the context of journalism, it is a reasonable application of the "principle of charity" in argument interpretation to presume that the information provided by the journalist constitutes a relatively complete picture of the relevant facts." In other words, the fact that the speaker was a journalist had a small role to play in the question.

It's possible to overthink these things. I got question 25, section 3 of LSAT Preptest 64 right, very fast. The answer was obvious. It was only when a student questioned me that I noticed a potential flaw. In 99.9% of cases you'll never need to consider relevant expertise. But know that the speaker's identity is explicitly part of LSAT questions.

Question 13

QUESTION TYPE: Weaken

CONCLUSION: We shouldn't feed animals GMO plants.

REASONING: Rats that ate GMO potatoes for 30 days had two problems. A control group fed a normal diet of foods did not develop these problems.

ANALYSIS: In a scientific experiment, you should keep variables the same, except the variable you're testing. The stimulus fails to do that. One group of rats eats only GMO potatoes. The other group eats "a normal diet". I'm pretty sure rats normally eat more than potatoes.

So the intestinal deformities could have been caused by the fact that rats weren't eating their normal diet, rather than because the potatoes were GMO.

A. **CORRECT.** This shows that the first group wasn't eating normal food. Maybe they got sick because rats don't digest potatoes well, and because they were missing foods they'd normally eat. Imagine eating nothing but potatoes!

B. You must always take answer choices at their weakest on weaken questions. "Tended to eat more" has a wide range of meanings. At it's weakest, it could mean that 51% of the rats ate 2% more potatoes at the start of the month. That doesn't tell us anything. (Though even if we took a stronger version of this answer, I'm not sure how it would weaken the argument!)

C. This affects nothing. The stimulus is talking about rats that *developed* intestinal deformities. The rats in the experiment were not the ones who had intestinal deformities at birth.

D. You might think that this shows that regular potatoes would have the same effect. But food is more than its nutritional value. "Has arsenic" is not a nutritional value – but you shouldn't eat an apple laced with arsenic! Maybe GMO potatoes have similar non-nutritional, poisonous effects.

E. You don't have to be able to explain something in order to warn against it. If 100% of people who eat a certain food die, then it's valid to say "don't eat it!!", even if you don't know why people die.

Question 14

QUESTION TYPE: Parallel Reasoning

CONCLUSION: It can't be true that we perceive an object by creating a mental image of the object.

REASONING: We'd need a new self to perceive the mental image. The inner self would need its own mental image, and this would go on to infinity.

ANALYSIS: This argument describes an infinite process. It's absurd to think our mind uses infinite process to form mental images, because infinite processes never end – we'd never get anything done!

This argument is hard to think about. Let that go. It's not your job to question the truth of premises. You must instead look for structure, and match it.

1. One thing requires a second thing.
2. The second thing requires another thing
3. This goes on forever.

In practice, you should simply look through the answers for a process that continues forever. Only the correct answer has such a process.

A. This answer doesn't describe an infinite process. Also note that this answer says "highly unlikely", while the stimulus said "*cannot* be correct."
B. This answer has the word infinite, but this answer describes an infinite *number* of theories. The stimulus described an infinite *process*. Those are different. For instance, an infinite process keeps going forever, referring back to itself. An infinite *number* of wrong theories already exist.
C. **CORRECT.** This answer describes an infinite process. Since *no* theory is new, every theory must have a similar theory that preceded it. This can't happen – obviously at some point a human thought up the first theory. So this infinite process is impossible, just like in the stimulus.
D. This answer has the word absurd, just like the stimulus. But you have to look at what "absurd" refers to. There is no infinite process here – the definition of "foundation" is simply wrong.
E. There's no claim of infinity here. This is just a factual argument that shows that some libraries existed before the library at Alexandria.

Question 15

QUESTION TYPE: Most Strongly Supported

FACTS:
1. You should not greatly exceed the recommended daily intake (RDA) of vitamins A and D – they are toxic.
2. Some vitamin fortified foods have 100% of the daily intake of those vitamins per serving.
3. Many people eat 2-3x the standard servings of some vitamin fortified foods.

ANALYSIS: We know "some" vitamin fortified cereals have 100% of the RDA. It's a warranted assumption that other vitamin fortified cereals have a significant percent of the RDA, say 30-50%.

We know some people eat 2-3x the recommended serving. And it's a warranted assumption that people get vitamin A and D from other food sources – everyone knows that.

This is just a most strongly supported question. It's probable, though not certain, that at least one person, somewhere in the world, has exceeded the RDA by eating lots of vitamin fortified cereal.

A. We don't know why people overeat cereal. Maybe they are aware of the RDA, and their mistake is simply about serving size.
B. **CORRECT.** At least some vitamin fortified foods have 100% of the daily intake. Presumably other such foods at least have high quantities of vitamins. Since "many" people eat large servings, and since they likely get some vitamin A and D from the rest of their diet, it's likely at least some people exceed the daily intake.
C. The only mistaken belief in the stimulus is how big a serving is. But people may pour cereal because they want to eat enough food – they may not be considering vitamin intake.
D. People may be deficient in certain vitamins even if they eat vitamin fortified foods. People might want to supplement those vitamins.
E. Manufacturers might not realize how people eat! Also, we only know vitamins A and D are toxic in extremely high doses. It's possible 2-3x the RDA is not a concern, and thus manufacturers don't need to worry about overeating.

Question 16

QUESTION TYPE: Necessary Assumption

CONCLUSION: It's likely that most countries that say their oil reserves haven't changed are wrong.

REASONING: A few countries say their reserves haven't changed last year. But oil reserves are unlikely to stay the same, year on year.

ANALYSIS: Notice the quantity words "several" and "most" in this stimulus. You must always pay attention to quantity words.

Several is perhaps 3-7 countries. And in the whole world, perhaps 100-150 countries have oil reserves. "Likely" might mean 70% of countries will see a change in reserves. So it's perfectly possible for it to be "unlikely" that oil reserves remain unchanged, and for 3-7 countries to have oil reserves that didn't change. 3-7 is a small percentage of the total. So the argument has to assume it's unlikely for this *group* to have its reserves unchanged.

A. **Negation:** "One country is likely to be right that its oil reserves are unchanged."
Who cares what happens in one country?
B. **CORRECT.** The conclusion is about "most" countries. If we negate this answer, we no longer have information about most countries that stated their reserves didn't change.
Negation: It is likely that only *half or less* of the countries which claimed unchanged reserves had oil fields that were drained or discovered.
C. We don't care *how* reserves change (e.g. slowly or quickly). We only care if they *did* change.
Negation: In 1997, no single country experienced both a a gradual drop and also a sudden rise in oil reserves.
D. Who cares what happens in one country?
Negation: One country incorrectly stated its reserves hadn't changed, but during 1997 it didn't discover new reserves or drain old ones.
E. This answer is irrelevant. We care about whether nations *are* correct, not whether they have an *obligation* to be correct.
Negation: A nation can experience changes in its oil reserves without having the obligation to report them correctly.

Question 17

QUESTION TYPE: Must be True

FACTS:
1. Sound insulate (SI)--> Quiet for home (Q)
2. Quiet for home (Q)--> Fine for institutions (I)
3. Combined statement: SI --> Q --> I
   Contrapositive: I̶ --> Q̶ --> S̶I̶
4. EM industries not quiet enough for home: Q̶
5. Inference: EM industries not sound insulated: S̶I̶

ANALYSIS: Usually, you should draw "must be true "questions, using letters. I kept the words in the first two statements so they're clear to you. But, the combined diagram above is how I actually draw.

After you make a diagram, the next step is to see how the fact about EM industries fits into the logical chain. Since EM is Q̶, then they must be S̶I̶. You can and *should* be 100% certain about this kind of deduction on must be true questions, before checking the answers.

A. This is an incorrect reversal of the first diagram.
B. **CORRECT.** This is true, according to the contrapositive diagram above.
C. We don't know. Being quiet enough for the home is a sufficient condition for being useful in institutional settings. EM fails to meet this sufficient condition. Failing to meet a sufficient condition doesn't tell you anything. It's possible some EM motors are quiet enough for institutions, or it's possible that none are.
D. This is an incorrect reversal of the first fact. Sound insulation guarantees quiet, but something could be quiet even if it's not insulated.
E. This is an incorrect negation of the second fact. Even if something is not quiet enough for use in the home, it might still be quiet enough for institutional settings.

Question 18

QUESTION TYPE: Flawed Reasoning

CONCLUSION: The factory won't cause health problems.

REASONING: The protestors complaining about health problems were sent by developers who were worried about the value of their land.

ANALYSIS: This is an ad hominem argument. The author attacks the motives of the protestors, in order to claim that their conclusion is wrong.

This is *never* correct. It's possible the factory poses a health risk – maybe that's why developers chose to highlight that issue rather than another concern!

You must always attack the evidence and reasoning of your opponent, never their identity.

A. The argument didn't do this.
   Example of Flaw: The protestors claim the factory will kill everyone in town. But it won't kill anyone.
B. The argument didn't do this either. Note that this isn't really a flaw: it's perfectly valid to persuade by pointing out harmful consequences.
   Example of Flaw: We must build the factory. Otherwise the local economy will fail and house prices will drop.
C. **CORRECT.** This answer choice describes an ad hominem flaw. The author didn't say the protestors were wrong, she just said they were biased.
D. It is a flaw to generalize from a small number of cases, but the argument didn't do this.
   Example of Flaw: The factory will make everyone sick. These two homeless orphans developed a cough while living near a similar factory.
E. This is a flaw, but the argument didn't do it.
   Example of flaw: You must admit that it's possible I'll win the lottery. Therefore it's 100% certain that I'll win the lottery.

Question 19

QUESTION TYPE: Principle

PRINCIPLE:

Should Intentionally misrepresent other's view (M)
--> Purpose is to act in interest of other (P)

Contrapositive: P̶ --> M̶

ANALYSIS: Principle questions make me angry. I'm angry at you right now for reading this. These questions are *soooo* easy, but people have trouble with them. Gah!

On principle questions, you must focus only on what you can conclude. You can only conclude necessary conditions. So on this question, you can conclude only *one* thing. If someone is misrepresenting the belief of another, then they should act in that person's interest. To violate the principle, they would *not* act in that person's interest.

So you're looking for *two* things:

1. Misrepresenting *someone else's* beliefs.
2. Purpose is not in the interest of that person.

If you get stuck, look at that list of *two* things. The wrong answer you're considering is missing one of them. Figure out what it is.

A. **CORRECT.** It's definitely against someone's interest to make them look ridiculous. This means that Ann shouldn't have misrepresented Bruce's beliefs.
B. Claude is acting in Thelma's interests: he is preventing someone from bothering her. No one likes being bothered.
C. John's purpose appears to be acting *for* Maria's interest: he wants people to respect her.
D. Harvey is misrepresenting *his own* beliefs.
E. It doesn't sound like Wanda is misrepresenting George's beliefs. He knows little about Geography, so maybe he doesn't know Egypt is in Africa. It's also not clear Wanda wants to harm George: maybe there is good reason to let people know the truth about his geographical limitations.

Question 20

QUESTION TYPE: Paradox

PARADOX: The family earned more from wool, but didn't get richer overall.

The family earned more from wool because they sold *much* more internationally, and international prices rose.

ANALYSIS: Several answers talk about low domestic wool prices. Who cares?! The family was selling *dramatically* more wool internationally. Besides, the first sentence *literally says* that the family earned more money from wool. A lot more money! There's *no* doubt about this.

So the family is poorer, *even though* they're raking in cash from wool. Use your common sense (you're allowed). If you sell wool, you have sheep. We use sheep for many things: meat, sheep's milk, cheese, etc. So it's quite likely that the family made money from these as well. Answer C says that the family lost money on non-wool sales.

A. The family wasn't selling as much wool domestically, so domestic wool prices don't matter. International wool prices sound like they were increasing faster than inflation.
B. This sounds tempting. But this family sold a *lot* more wool abroad, at higher prices. And the first sentence says that the family *earned more* from wool sales. There's zero doubt on that point.
C. **CORRECT.** This is the only answer that explains how wool sellers could lose money, even if they are making more money from wool. Maybe this family only made 30% of its money from wool, and the rest from sheepskin and mutton sales.
D. This talks about Australian wool producers in general. But the question is only about a specific family. This family is earning *lots* more from international wool sales. Presumably they're doing well even with the increased competition.
E. This answer doesn't explain why a wool farmer could lose money even though wool sales are increasing. Don't focus on whether an answer could be true – you need to pay attention to whether it explains the paradox.

Question 21

QUESTION TYPE: Flawed Reasoning

CONCLUSION: It wasn't wrong for Meyers to take the compost.

REASONING: The lawyer said Meyers didn't meet a sufficient condition for something being wrong.

ANALYSIS: This flaw question uses conditional reasoning. When a flaw questions uses conditional reasoning, there are only two possible errors. I'll use a sample sentence to demonstrate them: All cats have tails (C --> T)

- Incorrect negation (Not cat, so no tail C̶ --> T̶)
- Incorrect reversal (Has a tail, so is cat T --> C)

If you see conditional reasoning on a flaw question, assume they've done one of these two errors. Drawing isn't necessary. You just need to see whether they reversed or negated, then look for that answer. That said, here's the drawing:

Good reason --> Stealing --> Wrong
The lawyer incorrectly negated good reason: G̶ --> W̶

A. This is different. A fact is a fact. A moral judgment is an idea about a fact (e.g. it's good, it's bad, we should, we shouldn't)
   Example of flaw: You pointed out that millions of children are starving. How dare you say it is *fine* that millions of children are starving?
B. This answer describes a hypothetical situation. The lawyer was talking about what actually happened. The lawyer didn't say what would happen *if* Meyers thought the compost was someone's property.
C. **CORRECT.** This describes an incorrect negation. "A condition by itself enough...." is a sufficient condition. The argument assumed this sufficient condition was also necessary.
D. This isn't a flaw! If the compost was Meyers' property, it would have been fine for him to take it, and he wouldn't need a lawyer!
E. This is a different flaw.
   Example of flaw: Mrs. Jones said the compost was hers. This is possible. Therefore it is *certain* that the compost belongs to Mrs. Jones!

20

Question 22

QUESTION TYPE: Necessary Assumption

CONCLUSION: There's no problem with predatory pricing.

REASONING: The threat of competition will keep companies from raising prices, even if their competitors go out of business.

ANALYSIS: On necessary assumption questions, you must ask how the evidence could *fail* to justify the argument. What is the author assuming?

Here, they're assuming that competition would work. But if competitors *can't* enter the market, then this argument falls apart.

A. The argument said the *threat* of competition is what keeps companies from raising prices. Actual competition is not necessarily required.
   Negation: Some successful companies may avoid creating competitors.
B. "Unlikely" and "Likely" are related to most. Likely = 51%, unlikely = 50% or less. Since you must negate in the slightest way possible, negating unlikely means moving from 50% to 51%, which is never a significant change.
   Negation: It is likely that multiple companies will engage in predatory pricing.
C. Company size wasn't relevant. The issue is lack of competition. In a small market a company might drive out all competitors even if it isn't that big.
   Negation: At least one company that isn't large and wealthy can engage in predatory pricing.
D. Negating this makes the argument *stronger!* Additional reasons to avoid raising prices mean we don't need to worry about predatory pricing.
   Negation: There is at least one other reason companies avoid raising prices (e.g. Compassion, legal requirements, cost of changing ads, etc.)
E. **CORRECT.** The author assumed that prices are the only reason we should worry about predatory pricing. There could be other reasons. Maybe predatory pricing is not *fair* to competitors.
   Negation: Some pricing practices are unacceptable even if they do not result in unreasonable prices.

Question 23

QUESTION TYPE: Flawed Parallel Reasoning

CONCLUSION: Frank doesn't embezzle.

REASONING: Wants to prosecute --> Charged
~~Charged~~   ~~Embezzle~~

ANALYSIS: This argument gives a single conditional statement, then negates the necessary condition. We could have correctly concluded that the prosecutor doesn't want to prosecute Frank. But we don't know if Frank is an embezzler.

You could call it a concept shift. Prosecuting Frank for embezzlement doesn't mean Frank embezzles, and not prosecuting doesn't mean he is innocent.

A. This is a different error. It's a mistaken reversal:
   Knew --> 10
   Incorrect reversal: 10 --> knew
B. This is a different error. It's an incorrect negation
   Lottery --> stay home
   Incorrect negation: ~~lottery~~ --> ~~stay home~~
C. **CORRECT.** This argument correctly negates the necessary condition of a conditional statement. And then it repeats the concept shift error in the stimulus: we could conclude that Makoto does not *believe* the oven is on, but it's very possible that the oven is *actually* on. Belief ≠ fact, just like lack of prosecution ≠ innocence.
   Believe oven on --> Rush home
   Still at work. Therefore oven *actually* off.
D. This answer repeats the same concept shift error, moving from belief about getting a promotion, to *actually* getting a promotion. But, this argument makes an incorrect reversal. The stimulus correctly negated the necessary condition.
   Believed promotion --> Come in early
   Incorrect reversal: Come in early --> *actually* getting a promotion.
E. This repeats the belief/fact concept shift. However, the stimulus and answer C both negated the necessary condition of the conditional statement. This answer presents a flawed version of the sufficient condition.
   Believe going to be fired --> ~~come in to work~~
   Flawed sufficient condition: Lucy *is* going to be fired.

Question 24

QUESTION TYPE: Flawed Reasoning

CONCLUSION: Removing tonsils early will prevent all sleeping problems in children.

REASONING: Tonsils can sometimes cause sleeping problems, and removing them can help.

ANALYSIS: This is an awful argument. There are *thousands* of reasons a child could have sleeping problems. Removing tonsils eliminates *one* possible cause. Tonsils are not the *only* cause of sleep problems.

Something can be a cause without being a necessary cause.

A. The pediatrician is a *relevant* authority. And the pediatrician presents evidence; they are not asking us to take their word for it.
Example of flaw: I'm a wealthy industrialist. I feel that children should have their tonsils removed, so clearly I'm right.
B. This answer refers to circular reasoning. That's a different flaw – the evidence and the conclusion have to be *exactly* the same.
Example of flaw: Children would have no sleep problems if they had their tonsils removed, because removing tonsils eliminates sleep problems.
C. This is a different flaw.
Example of flaw: Removing tonsils reduces infections, and also reduces sleep problems. So clearly doctors that remove tonsils are intending to cure sleep problems and not just reduce infections.
D. This is a different flaw.
Example of flaw: One *possible* reason for removing tonsils is to reduce sleep problems. So clearly, *this child's* tonsils were removed to reduce sleep problems, and not for any other reason.
E. CORRECT. Maybe sleep problems are caused by fear of monsters under the bed, or playing too many video games late at night. There are a million-and-one reasons a child could have trouble sleeping, even if they have their tonsils removed.

Question 25

QUESTION TYPE: Principle

PRINCIPLE:
Knowledge not publicly available --> Unethical for officials to profit from knowledge

ANALYSIS: On logical reasoning questions, you must be *rigorous*. You must focus on *exactly* what condition allows you to prove a principle.

We have *one* sufficient situation for calling something unethical. Someone must:

1. Be a *current* government official, and
2. Use knowledge not publicly available, and
3. To benefit *themselves*
4. Financially

This is very similar to criminal law, where multiple conditions must be met for a crime. You must be rigorous and discard any answers that miss one of the above conditions.

Many answers describe situations where officials *might* be profiting. No good. We need definite proof that officials profited.

A. There's no evidence the official profited from his former company's bid. We don't even know that the bid succeeded. We also don't know if the official used knowledge that wasn't public.
B. This officer is a *retired* government official. The principle only applies to current officials.
C. It's not clear the official used knowledge that isn't available. She set up the shelters *after* the new law was passed.
D. CORRECT. This matches all four conditions. A current official used secret knowledge to benefit himself financially by avoiding a tax.
E. The official sold her stock *after* the investigation was announced, so there is no violation.

Section II - Logic Games
Game 1 - Film Schedule
Questions 1-5

Setup

This is a straightforward pure sequencing game. Except for the final question, there's absolutely nothing tricky here.

If you found this difficult, I have good news for you. This type of game is *very* learnable. Just redo it until it makes sense, and you'll be able to do *every* sequencing game with ease. Set high standards for yourself. A skilled LSAT student should be able to solve this in 4-5 minutes.

It's best to combine all the rules into one big diagram. I don't draw them separately. It is a waste of time, and in my experience it tends to confuse students. Better just to connect everything rule by rule. Here's the first rule:

```
   J
F<
   L
```

The second rule connects on J:

```
K
 >J—H
F<
   L
```

The third rule attaches on to L:

```
K
 >J—H
F<
   L—G
```

That's the entire setup. No need to make things more complicated than they are. The diagram reads left to right. Kangaroos or Fiesta could be first, as they have nothing before them. Hurricanes or Glaciers could be last, as they have nothing after them.

It's important to note that, for example, Jets could be before or after Glaciers. They're not directly connected, so there's no reason we can't put Glaciers before Jets, even though Glaciers is further right on the diagram.

Main Diagram

```
K
 >J—H
F<
   L—G
```

23

Question 1

Unusually for a first question, this is not an "acceptable order" question. That means the LSAT was expecting you to make deductions in your setup, such as the main diagram we created.

We're looking for what must be false. The slow way to do this question would be to test each answer choice and prove that it could work (thus eliminating it).

The fast way is to look through the answers to find the ones that seem more difficult. For instance, **A** is a poor candidate, because it places Fiesta early on. On our diagram, Fiesta is early: the only restrictions on Fiesta are that it goes *before* other variables. So it's easy to place Fiesta early, and **A** is unlikely to be correct.

It should be clear that **E** is **CORRECT**, once you have practice reading this type of diagram. Kangaroos comes before Jets and Hurricanes. That means that Kangaroos can go fourth at latest.

I'm going to show the other answers are all possible, but this isn't something you should do under timed conditions.

This diagram proves that **A** and **C** are wrong:

K	F	J	H	L	G
1	2	3	4	5	6

This diagram proves that **B** and **D** are wrong.

F	L	G	K	J	H
1	2	3	4	5	6

But I'll emphasize that this is not how you should solve this type of question. Rule violations on sequencing questions tend to be obvious.

Rule violations tend to happen when something is placed too near the edge. **e.g.** 5th is one space away from last, but Kangaroos always has to be at least two spaces away from last.

Question 2

K
 ⟍
  ⟍ J — H
F ⟨
  ⟋ L — G
 ⟋

I've repeated the main diagram. To solve "must be true" questions like this one, you should just look at the diagram to see what has to be true.

Fiesta is always before Hurricanes, so **A** is **CORRECT.**

None of the other answers have to be true. There are no left-to-right connections between the variables mentioned in those answers. A left-to-right connection is the only way you can prove one variable comes before another.

Question 3

The new rule on this question doesn't change much. If you find yourself hesitating, then it is best to redraw the diagram to add the new rule. This should only take 10 seconds or so. If it takes you longer, practice. Here's the diagram, with Glaciers before Hurricanes:

K
  \
    > J \
F <   H
  \   /
    L - G

The only real change is that Hurricanes now has to be last. Kangaroos and Jets could still go before Glaciers. So **A** is wrong. Glaciers could go as late as fifth.

E is CORRECT. Lovebird now has to have Glaciers and Hurricanes after it, so Lovebird can be fourth at latest.

Question 4

This question places Lovebird earlier than Kangaroos. I drew a new diagram showing this. I recommend trying this modification yourself. It's very quick to draw a new rule. Most students vastly overestimate how long it takes to make drawings.

          K — J — H
        /
F — L — G

From this diagram, it's obvious that **A, B** and **C** are wrong. Lovebird has to go second, since Kangaroos, Jets, Hurricanes and Glaciers come after Lovebird.

D is CORRECT. It not only could be true, it *has* to be true.

E is obviously wrong, as the diagram shows that Jets has to come *after* L.

Drawing the new diagram adds ten seconds, but likely saves you thirty seconds on the answer choices.

Question 5

This is the only question that most students find truly difficult on this game. Fewer than half got it right. Everyone hates rule substitution questions.

There is a way to do rule substitution questions quickly however. It's very difficult for the test makers come up with a new rule that has the same effect. Usually their only option is to describe the effects of the rule in another way. Let's see how to do that. Here's the main diagram again:

```
K
 \
  > J — H
 /
F
 \
  L — G
```

Now, let's look at the full effects of placing Fiesta before Jets and Lovebird.

- Fiesta is before J – H and L – G.
- Kangaroos is the only variable that can come before Fiesta.

I can think of two ways of phrasing this:

1. Every variable except Kangaroos has to come after F.
2. Only Kangaroos can come before F.

Answer **A** uses my second variation. **A** is **CORRECT.**

I think **B** and **D** are fairly obviously wrong. They both force something to happen that normally doesn't have to happen. Ordinarily, Kangaroos can come after Lovebird, so **B** is wrong. And normally, Kangaroos can come before Fiesta, so **D** is wrong.

C and **E** are trickier to eliminate. **C** is the most popular wrong answer. It places Fiesta first or second. It's true that Fiesta normally has to go in one of those positions. But that's not *all* that's true about Fiesta.

We also need the rule to force Fiesta to be before Lovebird, and answer **C** doesn't do that. The rule in answer **C** allows this scenario:

L	F	G	K	J	H
1	2	3	4	5	6

Fiesta is second, but Lovebird is before F!

E is the second most popular answer. It says that Fiesta or Kangaroos must be first.

E is also something that *has to be true* normally, but we're not looking for something that must be true. We're looking for something that replaces the rule. This scenario is possible if we replace the rule in question with answer **E:**

K	J	H	L	G	F
1	2	3	4	5	6

Kangaroos is first, but Fiesta is last! That violates the normal rules.

Game 2 - Applicants and Human Resources
Questions 6-11

Setup

This is a grouping game. I've set it up vertically. You can set this type of game up horizontally too. Either way is fine, depends how your brain works.

R __
S __
T __
U G

I've added G to group U. You should always read all the rules before drawing. Often one rule is very easy to draw and you should start there.

I next placed the final rule on the diagram:

R __
S __ __
T __
U G

The final rule says that S has more candidates than T, so S always has at least two candidates. The arrow reminds me that S has more than T. It's important to note that Tipton could evaluate at most two candidates. If Tipton evaluated three candidates, then Smith would have to evaluate four, and there would be no candidates left for the other two officers.

This is a non-standard rule, so you're welcome to use another symbol to remind yourself that S has more than T. But it's best if you can find a way to draw the rule directly on the diagram. The fewer rules in your list of rules, the better.

Next, is my list of rules. Here are rules 2, 3, and 4:

FL

I ⟨—+—⟩ M,H

K |

I've drawn rules 2 and 3 slightly differently. I normally prefer a box to show that variables must be or can't be in the same group. But that doesn't work for rule 3, so I used the dual arrow to show that Inman can't go with M or H.

The final rule has a vertical line to the right of K. That symbol means that the group K is in is closed: there can be no more candidates there. This type of rule occurs frequently enough that you should adopt this symbol.

Main Diagram

R __
S __ __
T __
U G

(1) FL

(2) I ⟨—+—⟩ M,H

(3) K |

Question 6

For acceptable order questions, go through the rules and use them to eliminate answers one by one.

Rule 1 eliminates **E.** Grant must be evaluated by Ullman.

Rule 2 eliminates **B.** Farrell and Lopez must be evaluated by the same officer.

Rule 3 eliminates **C.** Hong and Inman can't be evaluated by the same officer.

Rule 4 eliminates **D.** Kent must be evaluated alone.

A is **CORRECT.** It violates no rules.

Question 7

You should start local rule questions by drawing the new rule, then making a deduction. If Hong is evaluated by Rao, then Inman can't be evaluated by Rao:

```
I̶ R   H
   S   __  __
  ↙T
   U   G
```

Then you must ask yourself which of the remaining rules are affected by this new situation. Kent's rule is very important. Kent must always be alone, and now there is only one group where Kent can be alone. Kent must be evaluated by Tipton:

```
I̶ R   H
       __
   S   __  __
  ↙T   K|
   U   G
```

Once a diagram gets filled up, you should ask yourself who you can still place. Only FL and I,M are left, and IM can't go together.

We need two people to be evaluated by Smith, so FL must go there:

```
I̶ R   H        I ⟷ M
       __
   S   F   L
  ↙T   K|
   U   G
```

Only Inman and Madsen are left. They must go in different groups. They can go anywhere, except Inman can't go with Rao.

From this diagram, **B** is **CORRECT. B** could be true, and the diagram contradicts all the other answers.

Question 8

This question says that Tipton evaluates two candidates. And Rule five says that Smith must evaluate more candidates than Tipton does. So if Tipton evaluates two candidates, Smith must evaluate three candidates. That leaves one candidate for R and U:

R __ |
S __ __ __ |
T __ __ |
U G |

Next, look to the rules and see what applies. Kent must be alone in a group. That means Kent must be evaluated by Rao:

R K |
S __ __ __ |
T __ __ |
U G |

Just like on question 7, you must now see who's left to place. There's FL, and I, H and M. I, H and M can't go together. That means FL must be evaluated by Rao. This lets us separate I and HM.

R K |
S F L __ |
T __ __ |
U G |

I, H and M are left. Inman has to go with FL, because if Inman were evaluated by Tipton then either H or M would also be there. Next, since only Tipton has space left, both Hong and Madsen must go there:

R K |
S F L I |
T H M |
U G |

C is CORRECT. Farrell can't be evaluated by Tipton. All of the other answers have to be true.

This may seem like a lengthy process, but on the page it should take about 15 seconds. It takes a long time for me to write and for you to read because I'm going one step at a time, and I have to make sure what I'm doing is clear. But with practice, you can learn to see these steps intuitively in your head and do them quickly.

Question 9

This question says Madsen is evaluated alone. That means that there are two candidates who must be evaluated alone: Madsen and Kent.

Smith always evaluates at least two candidates, and Ullman always evaluates Grant. So that means that Rao and Tipton must evaluate Madsen and Kent.

Madsen and Kent are interchangeable on this question, I've drawn a line to show this. I use this type of line whenever an entire group is interchangeable:

```
   R   M|
  (  S        ___
   T   K|
     U   G
```

The next step is logically difficult. There are four people left to place: FL, H and Inman. H and Inman can't go together.

That means that one of H/I will go with FL. So these four variables will be distributed in a group of three and a group of one.

We need at least two people to go with Smith. So the group of three, the group with FL, must be evaluated by Smith:

```
   R   M|
  (  S   F   L   H/I
   T   K|
     U   G   I/H
```

Hong and Inman are interchangeable between Smith and Ullman.

B is **CORRECT.** Lopez must be evaluated by Smith.

Notice that all the other answers mention Madsen, Kent, Inman and Hong. These four variables are all interchangeable with another variable on this question, so they could never be the right answer.

Question 10

Farrell is always evaluated alongside Lopez (rule 2). This question adds Inman to the group, for a total of three candidates.

There are only two officers that can evaluate these three candidates: Rao and Smith. Tipton can't evaluate three candidates, because then Smith would have to evaluate four candidates.

And Ullman can't evaluate three *additional* candidates. Then Ullman would have four candidates, and there wouldn't be enough candidates left for Rao, Smith and Tipton. You need at least four candidates for those officers, since Smith always evaluates at least two.

So only Smith and Rao can handle FL and Inman. I drew a separate scenario for each possibility. If you practice making local scenarios, you should be able to do this in 15-20 seconds and then quickly solve the question.

First let's place FLI with Rao. Kent has to go with Tipton, because Kent has to be alone:

```
   R   F   L   I
  ,S          ___
  ↘T   K|
     U   G|
```

Only Hong and Madsen are left to place. They must be evaluated by Smith, since Smith must evaluate more candidates than Tipton does:

```
   R   F   L   I
  ,S   H   M
  ↘T   K
     U   G
```

Now let's place FLI with Smith:

```
 ┌R  ___
 │S  _F_  _L_  _I_
 └T  ___
  U  _G_
```

Rao and Tipton are the open groups, and they are interchangeable. Kent fills one of the groups. Now only Hong and Madsen are left to place. One of H/M goes with Rao or Tipton. The other H/M is flexible: they can go in the same group, or with Ullman:

```
 ┌R  H/M                H/M
 │S  _F_  _L_  _I_
 └T  _K_ |
  U  _G_
```

The line between Rao and Tipton is a reminder than H/M and Kent are interchangeable in this scenario.

In both diagrams it is impossible for Lopez to be evaluated by Ullman. **C is CORRECT.**

We have done more work than we had to. But if you practice, it shouldn't take you too long to make these scenarios, so the wasted effort doesn't matter. The scenarios will also help you prove definitively that the other answers could be true.

Question 11

As with all local rule questions, you should start by drawing the new rule. FL go with Rao:

```
 R  _F_  _L_
 ┌S  ___  ___
 └T  _K_ |
  U  _G_
```

I've placed Kent with Tipton. Kent must always be alone, and Tipton is the only officer left who can evaluate a single candidate.

Now we only have Madsen, Hong and Inman left to place. These three can't go together (rule 3). We also need to place at least two people with Smith (rule five).

Therefore, Madsen and Hong must go with Smith. Inman can go either with Rao or Ullman. Inman can't go with smith because of rule 3:

```
      R  _F_  _L_  ╲
 ⫽  ┌S  _H_  _M_ |  │ I
    └T  _K_ |        │
     U  _G_        ╱
```

E is CORRECT. We know where to place L, H, M, K, and G, for a total of five. (the question asks about *other* applicants).

Game 3 - Literature Course
Questions 12-16

Setup

This is a linear/sequencing game, with a second element: the courses are either summarized or not summarized.

I don't have any special approach for this type of game. I just mark summarized or not summarized under the diagram. Keep it simple.

(There will be examples summarized/not summarized diagram on the questions)

At first I thought this was just a sequencing game. I drew rules 3 and 4. Here's rule 3:

I then added rule 4:

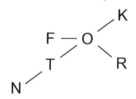

Most people would stop there. In fact, I did stop there on my own setup. But when I got to question 14, I noticed that this game is very restricted. Look at O. O is stuck in the middle. FTN are always before O, and KR are always after O.

So O is always fourth! This deduction makes the game *much* simpler. I redrew the sequencing rules as this diagram:

$$ \text{F , N} - \text{T} \qquad \text{K , R} $$
$$ \underset{\text{1}}{\quad} \; \underset{\text{2}}{\quad} \; \underset{\text{3}}{\quad} \; \underset{\text{4}}{\overset{\text{O}}{\quad}} \; \underset{\text{5}}{\quad} \; \underset{\text{6}}{\quad} $$

When I want to show semi-certain placement in a linear diagram, I draw some variables floating above the diagram. For instance, KR are always to the right of O. So I drew them in that position. The comma indicates that they are reversible.

I've done the same thing with " F, N – T ". N is always before T, but the comma indicates that F could be before them, after them or in the middle.

Drawing the diagram this way may seem like a small change. You might think "I could have figured all that out without the diagram!". But did you?

In any case, all logic games diagrams are just a tool to do things faster. This particular diagram let me fly through this game in six minutes. As much as possible, you should take knowledge out of your head, and put it on the page in the clearest possible form. You want to *always* know that O is fourth, without thinking about it.

There are two more rules. Courses can't go together if they're summarized. I drew it like this:

That's more of a reminder than anything else. I kept that rule in my head. Remembering it will help you go fast. You should always take 10-20 seconds at the start of a game to make sure you've memorized the rules.

The second rule says that if N is not summarized, then T and R are both summarized:

I only drew that. I've done enough logic games that the contrapositive is obvious to me. However, if it takes you time to see the contrapositive, then you should draw the contrapositive as well:

Main Diagram

F , N−T   K , R

$$\frac{}{1} \quad \frac{}{2} \quad \frac{}{3} \quad \frac{O}{4} \quad \frac{}{5} \quad \frac{}{6}$$

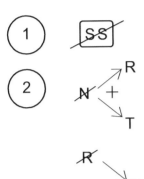

I don't draw the sequencing diagram I used in the setup. All that information is better captured in the first diagram I drew above.

Question 12

For acceptable order questions, go through the rules and use them to eliminate answers one by one.

Rule 1 eliminates **C**. T and R are summarized, so they can't go together.

Rule 2 eliminates **D**. N is not summarized, so R should have been summarized.

Rule 3 eliminates **B**. N has to be earlier than T.

Rule 4 eliminates **E**. F has to be earlier than O.

A is **CORRECT**. It violates no rules.

Question 13

If N is second, then T must go third, since N is always before T (rule 3).

$$K, R_S$$

$$\underline{F} \quad \underline{N} \quad \underline{T} \quad \underline{O} \quad \underline{} \quad \underline{}$$
$$1 \quad 2 \quad 3 \quad 4 \quad 5 \quad 6$$
$$ \quad \cancel{S} \quad S$$

The question also says that N is not summarized. This means that both T and R are summarized. (rule 2)

A is **CORRECT.** Since N is not summarized, there's no reason we can't summarize F.

B is wrong because K is beside R, and R is summarized.

C is wrong because O is beside T, and T is summarized.

D doesn't work on this question since N is second, and T must go after N.

E doesn't work because T is third, after N. And since N is not summarized, T must be summarized (rule 2).

Question 14

Not much changes on this question. O is summarized, so whoever goes 3rd and 5th can't be summarized. That's all we know:

$$F, \quad N-T \quad\quad K, R$$

$$\underline{} \quad \underline{} \quad \underline{} \quad \overset{O}{\underline{}} \quad \underline{} \quad \underline{}$$
$$1 \quad 2 \quad 3 \quad 4 \quad 5 \quad 6$$
$$ \quad \quad \cancel{S} \quad S \quad \cancel{S}$$

A and **B** are easy to eliminate. The diagram above shows that F can be first, and K can be sixth.

There are no summarization restrictions for these variables. A key to this game is that, except for N, you can *always* make a course not summarized.

C is **CORRECT.** It's a little tricky to explain. Try drawing this yourself.

If F is summarized, it can only go first or second, since no summarized course can go beside O on this question. Let's try placing F first. F is summarized, so the second course can't be summarized:

$$\quad\quad N-T \quad\quad K, R$$

$$\overset{F}{\underline{}} \quad \underline{} \quad \underline{} \quad \overset{O}{\underline{}} \quad \underline{} \quad \underline{}$$
$$1 \quad 2 \quad 3 \quad 4 \quad 5 \quad 6$$
$$S \quad \cancel{S} \quad \cancel{S} \quad \quad \cancel{S}$$

You may see the problem. We must place N and T second and third. Neither position can be summarized here. But if N isn't summarized, then T has to be summarized (rule 2). So this can't work.

The same problem happens if you place F second. N is first and T is third. Both positions can't be summarized, because they are beside F. But if N isn't summarized, then T must be summarized. We are breaking a rule:

$$\overset{N}{\underline{}} \quad \overset{F}{\underline{}} \quad \overset{T}{\underline{}} \quad \overset{O}{\underline{}} \quad \underline{} \quad \underline{}$$
$$1 \quad 2 \quad 3 \quad 4 \quad 5 \quad 6$$
$$\cancel{S} \quad S \quad \cancel{S} \quad S$$

This next diagram proves that **D** and **E** are both possible, and therefore wrong:

$$\boxed{\overset{N}{\underset{\cancel{S}}{}}} \quad \overset{T}{\underset{S}{}} \quad \overset{F}{\underset{\cancel{S}}{}} \quad \overset{O}{\underset{S}{}} \quad \boxed{\overset{K}{\underset{\cancel{S}}{}}} \quad \overset{R}{\underset{S}{}}$$
$$1 \quad 2 \quad 3 \quad 4 \quad 5 \quad 6$$

Question 15

If the final two courses are not summarized, then that means that R is not summarized, because R is one of the final two courses. We know this from our setup diagram: R is always fifth or sixth.

The contrapositive of rule 2 says that if R is not summarized, then N is summarized.

$$F, N_S - T \qquad K, R$$

$$\frac{}{1} \ \frac{}{2} \ \frac{}{3} \ \frac{O}{4} \ \frac{}{5} \ \frac{}{6}$$

There are a few ways we could place F, N and T. The most important thing is not to make two of them summarized and beside each other. Note that T could be summarized, if you place N first.

A is wrong. K is always fifth or sixth, so on this question it can't be summarized. **C** is wrong for the same reason.

B is **CORRECT**. This diagram shows that it's possible for O to be summarized:

$$\frac{F}{1} \ \frac{N}{2} \ \frac{T}{3} \ \frac{O}{4} \ \frac{K}{5} \ \frac{R}{6}$$
$$SS$$

D is wrong because if F and T are summarized, then the first three courses would all be summarized. This violates the first rule.

E is wrong because if R is not summarized, then N *must* be summarized.

Question 16

Everyone hates rule substitution questions, and this is the second on this section. Ouch.

I actually find rule substitution questions very easy. I'll try to convince you this is possible. There are two things a substituted rule must do:

1. *Allow* everything allowed by the old rule.
2. *Ban* everything not allowed by the old rule.

This gives you an easy way to eliminate answers. **A**, **B** and **E** add extra restrictions.

- **A:** This says T is discussed third. That doesn't normally have to be true. Wrong answer!
- **B:** This says T is discussed earlier than F. Not a normal restriction. Eliminate!
- **E:** This says F is discussed third. Normally, F can also go 1st or 2nd. Bad answer!

Have the courage of your convictions. Rule substitution answers are full of silly restrictions. If a restriction contradicts the normal rules, eliminate that answer.

Now we are left with **C** and **D**. The second part of my guidelines says that rules have to ban everything that's normally not allowed.

C doesn't do this. **C** says that K and R have to be among the last three. I'm sorry, but K and R have to be among the last *two*. This answer seems too broad. Let's look at **D**.

When I did this question, I went right to **D** because it said O has to be fourth. That's the most important deduction in the game, and it's also a consequence of the rule we're replacing.

Rule substitution answers usually work by describing a consequence of the rule we're replacing. **D** does describe a consequence of the rule (O is fourth), so this is very promising. Now let's see where this leaves us. O is fourth, and we know from rule 3 that N and T have to be before O.

(question continued on next page)

This diagram shows what we've deduced so far.

$$F, \widehat{KR}$$

$$N - T$$

$$O$$

$$\underline{\quad} \quad \underline{\quad} \quad \underline{\quad} \quad \underline{\quad} \quad \underline{\quad} \quad \underline{\quad}$$
$$1 \quad 2 \quad 3 \quad 4 \quad 5 \quad 6$$

We still have to place F and KR. This answer says that KR are beside each other and reversible. So they need two spaces.

The only two spaces open are 5 and 6. That means KR goes there, and F has to go before O. So this exactly matches our original setup. **D** is **CORRECT**.

I didn't prove this answer with this degree of certainty on the test. I just eliminated **A, B** and **E** like I showed you.

Then I discarded **C** because it said "last three", and I picked **D** because it placed O fourth. I did do a quick mental check that the rest of the rule worked, but those were the main elements I used to quickly arrive at the answer.

Game 4 - Seven Paintings
Questions 17-23

Setup

This is a linear game. I normally find linear games very easy, but this one was difficult. I even made a mistake on question 21, because I read the local rule wrong.

The setup diagram is pretty standard however. There are seven spaces, which we can draw horizontally. Since the Vuillard can only be third or fourth, I draw two diagrams. This only takes a few extra seconds, and it helps with visualization.

$$\underset{1}{\rule{0.6cm}{0.4pt}}\ \underset{2}{\rule{0.6cm}{0.4pt}}\ \overset{V}{\underset{3}{\rule{0.6cm}{0.4pt}}}\ \underset{4}{\rule{0.6cm}{0.4pt}}\ \underset{5}{\rule{0.6cm}{0.4pt}}\ \underset{6}{\rule{0.6cm}{0.4pt}}\ \underset{7}{\rule{0.6cm}{0.4pt}}$$

$$\underset{1}{\rule{0.6cm}{0.4pt}}\ \underset{2}{\rule{0.6cm}{0.4pt}}\ \underset{3}{\rule{0.6cm}{0.4pt}}\ \overset{V}{\underset{4}{\rule{0.6cm}{0.4pt}}}\ \underset{5}{\rule{0.6cm}{0.4pt}}\ \underset{6}{\rule{0.6cm}{0.4pt}}\ \underset{7}{\rule{0.6cm}{0.4pt}}$$

This dual setup isn't especially useful on this game, but on about 50% of games, dual diagrams produce incredible deductions. So I draw them out of habit, in case they produce something. Even if they don't, it only takes a moment, and I can visualize better by looking at them.

Next I drew rules 1-3, which are pretty standard.

Rule 1 says that the Turner is before the Whistler:

T—W

Rule 2 says that the Renoir is before the Morisot, with one painting in between:

R_M

Rule 3 says that the Pissarro and the Sisley are beside each other:

There are no major additional deductions from the setup. However, you should take some time to think about how the rules work together.

There are seven variables. The most restricted set of variables is R_M. Exactly one painting is in between them. Who can it be?

Not Pissarro or Sisley, because they are a block of two paintings. So only the Turner, the Whistler and the Vuillard can go in between the Renoir and the Morisot.

Games often present limited options, and it's important for you to think about the most restricted points in advance. The fact that only Turner, the Whistler and the Vuillard can go between R_M is very important.

Main Diagram

$$\underset{1}{\rule{0.6cm}{0.4pt}}\ \underset{2}{\rule{0.6cm}{0.4pt}}\ \overset{V}{\underset{3}{\rule{0.6cm}{0.4pt}}}\ \underset{4}{\rule{0.6cm}{0.4pt}}\ \underset{5}{\rule{0.6cm}{0.4pt}}\ \underset{6}{\rule{0.6cm}{0.4pt}}\ \underset{7}{\rule{0.6cm}{0.4pt}}$$

$$\underset{1}{\rule{0.6cm}{0.4pt}}\ \underset{2}{\rule{0.6cm}{0.4pt}}\ \underset{3}{\rule{0.6cm}{0.4pt}}\ \overset{V}{\underset{4}{\rule{0.6cm}{0.4pt}}}\ \underset{5}{\rule{0.6cm}{0.4pt}}\ \underset{6}{\rule{0.6cm}{0.4pt}}\ \underset{7}{\rule{0.6cm}{0.4pt}}$$

①　　T—W

②　　R_M

③　　PS

You could equally draw one diagram, and add a fourth rule that says V = 3 or 4. Whether or not you do this is personal preference. I do like having one fewer rule in my rule list.

Question 17

For acceptable order questions, go through the rules and use them to eliminate answers one by one.

Rule 1 eliminates **B.** The Turner must be closer to the entrance than the Whistler.

Rule 2 eliminates **A.** The Renoir must be closer to the entrance than the Morisot.

Rule 3 eliminates **D.** The Pissarro and the Sisley must be next to each other.

Rule 4 eliminates **E.** The Vuillard must be third or fourth, not second.

C is **CORRECT.** It violates no rules.

Question 18

This question places the Sisley in the seventh position. Whenever a question gives you a new rule, you can make an additional deduction.

Ask yourself which rules affect the Sisley. Rule 3 does: the Pissarro must be beside the Sisley. So the Pissarro must be in sixth on this question.

The Vuillard is the next variable I placed, since it can go third or fourth. I first tried putting the Vuillard third:

$$\frac{\quad}{1} \ \frac{\quad}{2} \ \frac{V}{3} \ \frac{\quad}{4} \ \frac{\quad}{5} \ \frac{P}{6} \ \frac{S}{7}$$

We needs three spaces for the Renoir and the Morisot, so they can only fit around the Vuillard:

$$\frac{\quad}{1} \ \frac{R}{2} \ \frac{V}{3} \ \frac{M}{4} \ \frac{\quad}{5} \ \frac{P}{6} \ \frac{S}{7}$$

In this diagram, the Turner could only go first, since the Turner has to go before the Whistler (rule 1). This doesn't help us, since "first" is not one of the answers.

So instead we can try putting Vuillard fourth:

$$\frac{\quad}{1} \ \frac{\quad}{2} \ \frac{\quad}{3} \ \frac{V}{4} \ \frac{\quad}{5} \ \frac{P}{6} \ \frac{S}{7}$$

R_M are the next hardest to place. They can only go first and third, or third and fifth (around the Vuillard).

It doesn't make sense to put them around the Vuillard, because then only spaces 1 and 2 would be open for the Turner and the Whistler. We already know the Turner can be in first place, and that's not the answer.

So let's place R_M first and third:

$$\frac{R}{1} \ \frac{\quad}{2} \ \frac{M}{3} \ \frac{V}{4} \ \frac{\quad}{5} \ \frac{P}{6} \ \frac{S}{7}$$

Here we can see that the Turner and the Whistler can go second and fifth:

$$\frac{R}{1} \ \frac{T}{2} \ \frac{M}{3} \ \frac{V}{4} \ \frac{W}{5} \ \frac{P}{6} \ \frac{S}{7}$$

So **A** is **CORRECT.** The Turner can go second.

38

Question 19

This is the last of the "easy" questions on this game. After this, people start making lots of mistakes.

If you got this wrong, it's worth sketching some diagrams on your own page to see how the rules work together. This question is testing whether you can visualize restrictions and interactions between rules. I'll walk you through how I did it. Bear in mind that this takes a lot of text to *explain,* but the process of drawing it on your page should only take 10-30 seconds.

If the Pissarro is fifth, then the Sisley can be fourth or sixth. I first tried fourth:

$$\frac{}{1} \quad \frac{}{2} \quad \frac{}{3} \quad \frac{S}{4} \quad \frac{P}{5} \quad \frac{}{6} \quad \frac{}{7}$$

Since the Vuillard can only be third or fourth, this means the Vuillard must go fourth:

$$\frac{}{1} \quad \frac{}{2} \quad \frac{V}{3} \quad \frac{S}{4} \quad \frac{P}{5} \quad \frac{}{6} \quad \frac{}{7}$$

This diagram doesn't work. We need three spaces for R_M, but in the diagram above there are only two consecutive spaces open.

So since the Sisley can't go fourth, it must go sixth. And that's the answer: **C is CORRECT.**

Whenever you're working on a question like this, you should always glance over the answers whenever you make a deduction. Often the first deduction you make will be the right answer.

Question 20

This is where the questions start to get hard. I think question 20, in particular, has the potential to slow you down, unnecessarily.

I have a secret. I skip questions like this. Then I keep them in the back of my mind. As I draw scenarios for other questions, I eliminate answers. By doing this you can often eliminate all but two answers, and you only have to draw a couple of diagrams to prove which answer is right.

The correct answer to question 17 proves that Morisot can go third, so **A** is wrong. Unfortunately, none of the other questions produced scenarios that disproved answers here. Still, eliminating one answer is a good way to start.

I recommend making very rapid sketches to disprove the other answers. Do this before reading the rest of my explanation – this is a good review exercise. It shouldn't take long, and you often don't need to complete a sketch on the page to see that a scenario would work.

For instance, here's **B,** in two steps:

Step 1:

$$\frac{}{1} \quad \frac{}{2} \quad \frac{R}{3} \quad \frac{V}{4} \quad \frac{M}{5} \quad \frac{}{6} \quad \frac{}{7}$$

Step 2:

$$\frac{P}{1} \quad \frac{S}{2} \quad \frac{R}{3} \quad \frac{V}{4} \quad \frac{M}{5} \quad \frac{T}{6} \quad \frac{W}{7}$$

Remember, these diagrams only have to prove that something *could* be true. In the diagram above, PS could be reversed, but who cares? Either way, the diagram proves the Renoir can be third.

(question continued on next page)

Here's **C,** in two steps:

Step 1:

$$\frac{\quad}{1} \quad \frac{P}{2} \quad \frac{S}{3} \quad \frac{V}{4} \quad \frac{\quad}{5} \quad \frac{\quad}{6} \quad \frac{\quad}{7}$$

Step 2:

$$\frac{T}{1} \quad \frac{P}{2} \quad \frac{S}{3} \quad \frac{V}{4} \quad \frac{R}{5} \quad \frac{W}{6} \quad \frac{M}{7}$$

Here's **D,** in three steps.

Step 1:

$$\frac{\quad}{1} \quad \frac{\quad}{2} \quad \frac{T}{3} \quad \frac{V}{4} \quad \frac{\quad}{5} \quad \frac{\quad}{6} \quad \frac{\quad}{7}$$

Step 2:

$$\frac{\quad}{1} \quad \frac{\quad}{2} \quad \frac{T}{3} \quad \frac{V}{4} \quad \frac{R}{5} \quad \frac{\quad}{6} \quad \frac{M}{7}$$

Step 3:

$$\frac{P}{1} \quad \frac{S}{2} \quad \frac{T}{3} \quad \frac{V}{4} \quad \frac{R}{5} \quad \frac{W}{6} \quad \frac{M}{7}$$

Note that these don't take long at all. I just try putting T third, then see what else has to be true, and then finally what can be true. Here are the steps to prove that T can be third:

- T third
- V must be fourth
- R_M must be 5 and 7
- PS must be 1 and 2 (or vice-versa)
- W must be 6

Since the diagram works, you can eliminate that answer. I'll emphasize that if you *practice* doing this, and you know the rules, it should take 5-10 seconds to go through the steps above.

By process of elimination, **E** is **CORRECT.** Here's why, there's no space for PS:

Step 1:

$$\frac{\quad}{1} \quad \frac{\quad}{2} \quad \frac{W}{3} \quad \frac{V}{4} \quad \frac{\quad}{5} \quad \frac{\quad}{6} \quad \frac{\quad}{7}$$

Step 2:

$$\frac{T}{1} \quad \frac{\quad}{2} \quad \frac{W}{3} \quad \frac{V}{4} \quad \frac{R}{5} \quad \frac{\boxed{PS}?}{6} \quad \frac{M}{7}$$

Now, you're probably saying to yourself "I don't have time to make all those drawings!". Actually, you do. There are three problems:

1. You overestimate how long it actually takes you to draw.
2. You haven't practiced drawing quickly.
3. You don't know the rules well enough.

I did those sequences of drawings on paper first. Each one took me about five seconds. Here's the steps:

1. Place the variable in the answer choice third.
2. Place Vuillard fourth.
3. Place R_M, the next most restricted element.
4. Place PS.
5. Place W after T.

None of that should take long. It should be automatic. Step 1, step 2, step 3, step 4, step 5, bam!

Improving is simple. On review, practice making these drawings until you are blazing fast at it. This skill will transfer over to new games.

Question 21

In the setup I said that only the Turner, the Whistler and the Vuillard can go between R_M. This question restricts R_M further. Since Turner must go before R_M and Whistler must go after, only Vuillard is left to go between.

There are two scenarios, since Vuillard can go third or fourth. Let's build both at once. This is how I sketched it on my page:

$$\underset{1}{\_} \quad \underset{2}{R} \quad \underset{3}{V} \quad \underset{4}{M} \quad \underset{5}{\_} \quad \underset{6}{\_} \quad \underset{7}{\_}$$

$$\underset{1}{\_} \quad \underset{2}{\_} \quad \underset{3}{R} \quad \underset{4}{V} \quad \underset{5}{M} \quad \underset{6}{\_} \quad \underset{7}{\_}$$

RVM are a block. The question says that we have to place Turner and Whistler before and after this block. In the first diagram, Turner must go first, and Whistler goes after, along with PS:

W, PS

$$\underset{1}{T} \quad \underset{2}{R} \quad \underset{3}{V} \quad \underset{4}{M} \quad \underset{5}{\_} \quad \underset{6}{\_} \quad \underset{7}{\_}$$

The other diagram, with Vuillard fourth, doesn't work. Once we place Turner and Whistler, there is no place to put the PS block:

PS ?

$$\underset{1}{\_} \quad \underset{2}{T} \quad \underset{3}{R} \quad \underset{4}{V} \quad \underset{5}{M} \quad \underset{6}{W} \quad \underset{7}{\_}$$

(Turner doesn't have to go second, I just placed it there to illustrate that this doesn't work)

So only the other scenario works. We can use this to eliminate answers.

W, PS

$$\underset{1}{T} \quad \underset{2}{R} \quad \underset{3}{V} \quad \underset{4}{M} \quad \underset{5}{\_} \quad \underset{6}{\_} \quad \underset{7}{\_}$$

The diagram contradicts **B** through **E**. **E** is wrong because if Whistler were sixth then there'd be no way for PS to be beside each other.

A is **CORRECT.** Pissarro could go fifth. This scenario proves it:

$$\underset{1}{T} \quad \underset{2}{R} \quad \underset{3}{V} \quad \underset{4}{M} \quad \underset{5}{P} \quad \underset{6}{S} \quad \underset{7}{W}$$

Question 22

Less than half of students get this question right. To do this question well, you have to be comfortable with making quick drawings to see what's possible.

Let's look at who we have to place for this question:

1. V, which goes third or fourth
2. PS, which go together
3. R_M, which form a block of three
4. T_W, which form a block of three

Apart from V, there is no variable that just takes up one space! That's very restrictive.

Once you see these are the restrictions, you must draw it. This is not the time for hesitation. I've seen students waste 40-60 seconds trying to work things out in their heads. This does not work! You will learn more in five seconds of drawing than ninety seconds of thinking. Watch this progression of drawings where I try to make a correct scenario with Vuillard fourth:

$$\underset{1}{\underline{\quad}} \ \underset{2}{\underline{\quad}} \ \underset{3}{\underline{\quad}} \ \underset{4}{\underline{V}} \ \underset{5}{\underline{\quad}} \ \underset{6}{\underline{\quad}} \ \underset{7}{\underline{\quad}}$$

$$\underset{1}{\underline{R}} \ \underset{2}{\underline{\quad}} \ \underset{3}{\underline{M}} \ \underset{4}{\underline{V}} \ \underset{5}{\underline{T}} \ \underset{6}{\underline{\quad}} \ \underset{7}{\underline{W}}$$

PS ?

$$\underset{1}{\underline{R}} \ \underset{2}{\underline{\quad}} \ \underset{3}{\underline{M}} \ \underset{4}{\underline{V}} \ \underset{5}{\underline{T}} \ \underset{6}{\underline{\quad}} \ \underset{7}{\underline{W}}$$

I put Vuillard fourth, and I placed the three remaining blocks. You can switch the order of R_M and T_W, but the result is the same: we're missing the two open spaces required for PS.

So let's try putting Vuillard third. Again, I'll show the progression of my sketch:

$$\underset{1}{\underline{\quad}} \ \underset{2}{\underline{\quad}} \ \underset{3}{\underline{V}} \ \underset{4}{\underline{\quad}} \ \underset{5}{\underline{\quad}} \ \underset{6}{\underline{\quad}} \ \underset{7}{\underline{\quad}}$$

$$\underset{1}{\underline{P}} \ \underset{2}{\underline{S}} \ \underset{3}{\underline{V}} \ \underset{4}{\underline{\quad}} \ \underset{5}{\underline{\quad}} \ \underset{6}{\underline{\quad}} \ \underset{7}{\underline{\quad}}$$

$$\underset{1}{\underline{P}} \ \underset{2}{\underline{S}} \ \underset{3}{\underline{V}} \ \underset{4}{\underline{R}} \ \underset{5}{\underline{T}} \ \underset{6}{\underline{M}} \ \underset{7}{\underline{W}}$$

I made this to prove that Vuillard can go third: it's a way of confirming that we were right to think that Vuillard can't go fourth.

This is just a could be true scenario. I know that PS can reverse positions, and R_M and T_W can also reverse positions. You don't need to draw every possible scenario for a diagram to be useful.

Since PS, R_W and T_W can all switch positions, none of those letters are possible candidates for something that must be true. That leaves Vuillard. We saw that Vuillard can't go fourth, so Vuillard must go third. **E is CORRECT.**

Question 23

Remember in the setup I said that only the Turner, the Vuillard, and the Whistler can go between the Renoir and the Morisot?

This restriction is rather central. In this question, the Turner is beside the Vuillard. That means that neither the Turner nor the Vuillard can go in between R_M. So only Whistler can.

Once you make a deduction like that, it usually answers the question. **B** is **CORRECT.** The Renoir must always come before the Whistler, because they go in this order: RWM

This may not be a satisfactory explanation for this question. That's the trouble with questions like this. Either they take forever, and you solve them with brute force, or you solve them quickly.

I personally didn't figure out the solution in advance. I make one scenario with the Turner next to the Vuillard. In the process of drawing, I noticed that the Renoir had to be before the Whistler, and *at that point* I realized there was no other way.

Making drawings is a revelation. You see things you could never possibly realize if you just try to think a question through. If I can teach you one thing, it's this: practice drawing, rather than thinking.

I'll repeat that, because it's important. Instead of thinking: draw, and draw quickly. In the process of drawing, you will figure things out.

To draw well, and fast, you need to know the rules. There's no substitute for this.

Section III - Logical Reasoning

Question 1

QUESTION TYPE: Flawed Reasoning

CONCLUSION: TekBank is more expensive than GreenBank.

REASONING: GreenBank has free ATMs. TekBank charges for its ATMs.

ANALYSIS: You're allowed to use common sense to form hypotheses on the LSAT. You *know* from your everyday life that banks have many fees. ATM fees are just a small part of the costs of having an account.

So TekBank could be cheaper than GreenBank if TekBank has no monthly fees, no overdraft fees, etc.

A. This is not a flaw (in this case)! The conclusion is only about an economic factor (cost), so it's appropriate for the evidence to only involve economic factors.
   Example of flaw: GreenBank will make you happy, because GreenBank is inexpensive.
B. This didn't happen.
   Example of flaw: GreenBank is better. A teller at a Chicago branch of TekBank insulted me once, three years ago!
C. **CORRECT.** Here we go. To make a proper comparison, we'd have to know that GreenBank was at least as affordable as TekBank in other respects as well, such as monthly fees.
D. This is a different flaw.
   Example of flaw: Overall, GreenBank is a friendly bank to deal with. So this particular GreenBank teller, Grumpy Bob, is surely friendly.
E. This is a different flaw.
   Example of flaw: There is no evidence that TekBank offers better interest rates than GreenBank. So it must not be true that TekBank offers better interest rates.

Question 2

QUESTION TYPE: Point At Issue

ARGUMENTS: Klein argues that Einstein's theory is wrong. We have only found 1/10th of the matter predicted by the theory.

Brown argues that the theory has been successful in other areas, so it's more sensible to conclude that the theory is correct, and that we simply haven't found the remaining 9/10ths of matter.

ANALYSIS: For point at issue questions, the right answer must meet two criteria:

1. Both people have an opinion about the answer.
2. The opinions are different.

Most answers fail the first test, because only one author has an opinion about the answer.

A. Both Klein and Brown *agree* this is true.
B. Klein doesn't mention whether Einstein's theory has had successes.
C. Neither Klein nor Brown says whether an acceptable alternate theory exists at present.
D. **CORRECT.** Klein agrees. Brown thinks instead that we simply haven't found all the matter.
E. Both Klein and Brown seem to accept that current estimates of matter found are accurate.

44

Question 3

QUESTION TYPE: Paradox

PARADOX: Chimpanzee anger can lead to both threat gestures and attacks. But threat gestures are rarely followed by attacks, and attacks rarely are preceded by threat gestures.

ANALYSIS: You might wonder why the stimulus says *both* of these things:

- Attacks rarely come after threat gestures.
- Attacks are rarely preceded by threat gestures.

These sound similar, but they are *very* different. The first refers to the odds of an attack, *if* you have a threat gesture. The second refers to the odds that a threat gesture occurred, *if* there was an attack.

Let's imagine two situations:

- 1,000 threat gesture incidents, 10 attacks, all attacks preceded by threat gestures
- 1,000 threat gesture incidents, 500 attacks, only 30 attacks preceded by threat gestures

In the first situation, it's true that attacks rarely come after threat gestures. But attacks are *always* preceded by threat gestures. So the first situation contradicts the second fact.

The second situation is consistent with both facts. Attacks rarely come after threat gestures. And threat gestures rarely come before attacks.

A. This explains why chimps make threat gestures, but it doesn't explain why chimps don't attack.
B. **CORRECT.** Threat gestures prevent chimps from having to make attacks. This explains why attacks rarely are preceded by threat gestures – if the chimps *had* made threat gestures then they wouldn't have felt angry enough to attack.
C. Suppose chimpanzees also display aggression by making funny faces. How does that explain anything about attacks and threat gestures?
D. This doesn't explain why chimpanzees don't attack after making threat gestures.
E. Tempting, but this statement doesn't *explain* why threat gestures don't lead to attacks. This is just a fact about chimpanzees.

Question 4

QUESTION TYPE: Strengthen

CONCLUSION: The Magno-Blanket can probably reduce pain in arthritic dogs.

REASONING: A study showed that patients reported reduced pain after being treated with Magno-Blankets. Dogs are similar to humans with respect to how close the blankets will be to their joints.

ANALYSIS: The LSAT expects you do know the basics of the scientific method. Every study should have a control group. Otherwise, your treatment method may be a placebo, or your results may be due to another factor.

For example, people might have felt reduced pain because they received human contact and attention from the doctors conducting the study. Or maybe the belief that they were being treated made the patients less stressed, and therefore better able to heal their pain.

Notice the study only says patients *reported* reduced pain. This level of detail is important. If the study *showed* that patients had a reduction in pain, then the argument would be stronger, as presumably a study has a control group if it *shows* a result.

A. Who cares about cats? We're trying to strengthen the idea that the blanket will help dogs. It doesn't matter what the blanket does to other animals.
B. This sounds pretty good, but it doesn't tell you that magnets reduce pain. In fact, *pain* is a signal transmitted from nerve cells to brains. So this answer could mean that magnets *increase* pain.
C. This answer suggests that it is *important* that we find a solution for dog pain. But this answer doesn't tell us that magno-blankets will *work*.
D. This is just a fact about who experienced the biggest benefit. We don't care who gets the most out of magnets. We only care if the magnets work, period.
E. **CORRECT.** This shows that the study followed the scientific method. Studies need control groups to be valid.

Question 5

QUESTION TYPE: Complete the Argument

CONCLUSION: The argument will likely say that there we haven't proven advertising is bad.

REASONING: Art and music changes people's preferences, and we think they are fine. Advertising also changes people's preferences.

ANALYSIS: This is a "complete the argument" question; you do not need to be critical or find flaws.

Instead, you need to understand how the author makes their case. This is an argument by analogy. The author mentions art and music classes because they are similar to advertising. So the author will conclude that advertising is fine, just like those classes.

The author agrees that advertising can change preferences. Their point is that this is not necessarily bad, since music and art classes do the same thing, and those classes are ok.

Notice the word "however". This means the author disagrees with the first sentence.

A. This answer is a factual statement about how much advertising changes preferences. The author isn't concerned with the degree of preference shift. Her point is that the preference shift doesn't matter.
B. Nonsense. The author *doesn't* think advertising is pernicious (bad). She mentions art and music classes to prove that advertising is acceptable.
C. **CORRECT.** Art and music classes change preferences, and we don't think they are bad. So if advertising is bad, it's not simply because it changes preferences.
D. This goes too far. The author didn't say advertising is good. She just pointed out that we can't say it is bad merely because it changes preferences, since art and music classes also change preferences.
E. The stimulus contradicts this answer. Music and art classes *do* change people's preferences. The author appears to agree that advertising changes preferences.

Question 6

QUESTION TYPE: Principle

CONCLUSION: High school counsellors should tell students what life is like for local newspaper reporters.

REASONING: Most journalists work for local newspapers. High school students interested in journalism imagine a life of glamour.

ANALYSIS: Notice that the conclusion says what counselors "should" do. On the LSAT, you can *never* assume anyone "should" do anything. For example, this is *not* a good argument, even though everyone would agree with it.: "We can save these kittens from a burning building at no risk to ourselves. So we should save those kittens".

We need to add the principle "you should save kittens, if you can do so without risking your health". Making that underlying principle *explicit* supports the argument. We must find a similar principle for this question. The argument says we should tell these kids the truth. Why would someone think that is a good idea? They must believe something like "if you can correct a mistaken impression, you should".

A. The most tempting wrong answer. The conclusion is only that we should tell students what journalism is like. The argument didn't say we should *discourage* students.
B. The conclusion was about telling the truth, not about encouraging people to seek goals. And where did maximizing the chance of a happy life come from?
C. This doesn't match the stimulus. The conclusion wasn't that we should encourage people to be international reporters. It was that we should let them know most reporters aren't international.
D. **CORRECT.** This is the most complex answer. Never ignore an answer because it uses big words! "disabuse of unrealistic conceptions" = make sure the students know the truth.
E. Tempting, but we have no idea if local journalists regret their choice. It's true that high school students want to be international journalists. But maybe once they become local journalists they'll realize it's actually quite fun.

Question 7

QUESTION TYPE: Flawed Reasoning

CONCLUSION: The "safety" features are useless.

REASONING: Most pedestrian injuries happen at cross-walks with "safety" features.

ANALYSIS: This argument mixes up relative and absolute. Safety features improve *relative* safety. That means they make you safer.

Meanwhile, the safety of the crosswalks is absolute. They are either "safe" or "unsafe". So, the crosswalks in question could be *extremely* dangerous (an absolute measure). That's why they have safety features. The features make them *safer,* but not *safe.*

My explanation may seem rather abstract, but once you grasp this relative/absolute difference, you'll see it *everywhere.* Think deeply about this one. Here are some examples.

"You are *safer* with a fire extinguisher in a burning building, but you are not *safe."*

"You are *less* healthy if you skip the gym one week, but you are probably not *unhealthy."*

————————————

A. **CORRECT.** If the safety features are placed only at the most dangerous intersections, then maybe those intersections would be even more dangerous without the features.
B. This isn't a flaw! If a safety feature really did fail to prevent injuries, why would we want it?
C. The argument didn't say this! No other safety features were mentioned. For a flaw answer to be correct, it has to happen.
D. Think about what this answer *really* means. It's insane. If the sidewalks in question have *no* other safety features, that means that every sidewalk in the country with stripes and flashing lights literally has *no* other features, such as a crosswalk sign.
The author didn't assume this, and I don't know why they would. You have to take answers literally. This one is rather extreme.
E. Totally irrelevant. The author doesn't say anything about injuries to drivers.

Question 8

QUESTION TYPE: Strengthen

CONCLUSION: The Korean aurora borealis helps confirm that John of Worcester saw sunspots.

REASONING: Sunspots typically produce an aurora borealis, after five days. Koreans observed an aurora borealis five days after John of Worcester claimed he saw sunspots.

ANALYSIS: This seems like a good argument. There is no horrendous flaw. The conclusion is appropriately mild: it just says the Korean sighting *helps* confirm John's claim.

To strengthen the argument, we can simply make the confirmation stronger. As things stand, it's possible that some other element caused the aurora borealis. The right answer shows that *only* sunspots could have caused the aurora.

————————————

A. This *weakens* the claim by showing the aurora borealis might have occurred even if John's sighting was false.
B. Nonsense. The argument didn't claim John was the first person to see sun spots. The author just said John *did* see sunspots, so it doesn't matter who else saw them on a previous occasion.
C. **CORRECT.** This virtually guarantees the conclusion. It eliminates the possibility that the aurora borealis had another cause. Therefore there was heavy sunspot activity on the day that John of Worcester claimed to have seen sunspots.
D. This weakens the argument, by adding necessary conditions to John of Worcester's claim. We don't know if John met these necessary conditions.
E. This is just a neat fact. We're trying to prove that John did see sunspots. These illustrations don't prove anything. In fact, if John *didn't* see sunspots, then these illustrations are false.

Question 9

QUESTION TYPE: Principle

CONCLUSION: If you want to improve society, then you shouldn't believe that individuals can't affect it.

REASONING: If you don't think individuals can affect society, you will feel too helpless to change it.

ANALYSIS: On LSAT principle-justify questions, you must first of all figure out what the argument is saying. Let's look at the logic. It boils down to this:

"If you think individuals are powerless, then you'll turn into a helpless loser and you won't accomplish anything. Therefore you *shouldn't* believe that individuals are powerless."

Notice the word "should" in the conclusion. On the LSAT, you can *never* prove that something "should" happen unless you have a premise that says what you "should" do. So we need a "should" statement that links the premise and the conclusion. Like this:

"If something makes you a helpless loser, then you *shouldn't* believe it."

A. This doesn't match the conclusion, which was about what you should *believe*.
B. We're trying to prove that individuals *should* reject the belief that historical forces determine the future. This answer tells us what people should do *if* they reject this belief.
   So this refers to the wrong term. This is an *extremely* common technique for tricky answers.
C. Like answer B, this refers to the wrong thing. This answer talks about what you should do *if* you already feel helpless. We must prove that you *should avoid* beliefs that make you feel helpless.
D. **CORRECT.** If this is true, then you shouldn't accept the belief that society is determined by vast historical forces. We know that would make you feel too helpless to improve society.
E. Rubbish. The stimulus was about what we should *believe*, not how we should *act*.

Question 10

QUESTION TYPE: Must Be True

FACTS:

1. Subcontract --> Lose control
2. **Contrapositive:** ~~Lose control~~ --> ~~Subcontract~~
3. The company only subcontracts with companies that maintain control

ANALYSIS: We have a conditional statement (Facts 1 and 2) and a fact (fact 3). You can combine them. The stimulus says that the companies the president uses for outsourcing don't lose control. According to the contrapositive above, those companies therefore don't subcontract.

Several wrong answers bring in outside assumptions about outsourcing being poor quality. The stimulus doesn't support this. If you outsource, you lose *control* over quality, but that doesn't necessarily mean the quality is lower. It just means you don't *control* whether or not quality is high.

A. **CORRECT.** This must be true. If the subcontractors were allowed to subcontract, then they would lose some control. Since the subcontractors *don't* lose control, we know they don't subcontract.
B. The stimulus never talks about disappointment. This answer is trying to make you bring in outside assumptions about outsourcing and poor quality.
C. This has to be *false*. If the company's president wanted full control, then they wouldn't outsource. You always lose control when you outsource.
D. This is similar to B. This might be true in real life, but nothing in the stimulus tells us that subcontracting leads to poor quality. We only know it leads to loss of control, which is not the same thing.
E. Careful. Loss of control doesn't necessarily mean loss of quality. We only know subcontracting leads to less control.
   Also note that this says *uniformly* better quality. That's a strong statement – it means every single in house product is better (i.e. there are zero duds).

Question 11

QUESTION TYPE: Sufficient Assumption

CONCLUSION: If students don't achieve broad mastery, they aren't being taught using appropriate methods.

REASONING: Students achieve broad mastery if they are taught with appropriate methods and they devote significant effort to their studies.

ANALYSIS: This is an unusually tricky sufficient assumption question. To get this right, you really need to draw it and see the flaw first. In fact I'm going to draw it like a logic game.

This is a *long* explanation. However, when I did this question myself, I did it rather quickly. The reason is that this process takes a long time to *explain,* but this process does not take a long time to *do.*

You should use this explanation to understand, but then practice the diagramming process on your own so that you learn it and can apply it quickly.

First let's look at the conclusion. We need to get from lack of broad mastery to lack of appropriate methods:

$$\not B \longrightarrow \not M$$

Now let's look at the evidence. If you have appropriate methods AND significant effort, you have broad mastery:

The contrapositive is that if you don't have broad mastery, you're missing appropriate methods or significant effort:

And this is where the flaw is. If we lack broad mastery, it's possible we have appropriate methods, and the problem is that we lack significant efforts. Not good. We need to make it 100% certain that lack of broad mastery means no appropriate methods.

There are two possibilities when you lack broad mastery: $\not M$ or $\not E$. We can guarantee the conclusion by showing that either possibility leads to $\not M$.

If we say that all appropriate methods lead to effort (M --> E), then this attaches on to the diagram as the contrapositive ($\not E$ --> $\not M$):

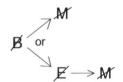

Now this matches the conclusion. If we don't have broad mastery, then we don't have adequate methods, no matter which path we choose.

Note: My diagrams are just one letter. If you make long, confusing acronyms, your own diagrams will destroy you. I've seen this happen time and time again. Diagrams are just a tool. The real knowledge should be in your head. Pick one useful letter, and *remember* what the letters refer to.

Note: I didn't do this diagram the first time I did this question. I solved this question with intuition. But following these steps will help improve your conditional logic, and there will be easier questions that you *can* solve up front.

(Discussion of answer choices on next page)

A. CORRECT. See the explanation above. This answer matches the addition statement I added to the diagram, and proves the conclusion. If this is true, then lack of broad mastery inevitably leads to lack of adequate methods.

B. This is a reversal of part of the evidence: broad mastery --> significant efforts.
We're looking for something that tells us what happens if we *don't* have broad mastery.
The "even if" part of this answer choice is meaningless fluff, it means that appropriate methods are neither sufficient nor necessary.

C. This tells us: broad mastery --> appropriate methods. That's a reversal of the evidence from the argument, where appropriate methods were part of a sufficient condition for broad mastery.
Contrapositive of the answer: ~~appropriate methods~~ --> ~~broad mastery.~~
Not helpful. We need an answer that tells us what happens if we *don't* have broad mastery. It needs to b the sufficient condition: e.g. ~~broad mastery~~ --> [something useful].

D. So? This was already implied by the stimulus. We only know that appropriate methods are a sufficient condition if they are accompanied by effort.

E. This is the same as D. We already know this is true. Efforts are only sufficient if accompanied by appropriate methods.

Question 12

QUESTION TYPE: Identify The Conclusion

CONCLUSION: The heavier can doesn't necessarily have more food.

REASONING: The heavier can could simply have more water.

ANALYSIS: The conclusion is the first sentence: the heavier can may not have more food. There are at least three ways to identify the conclusion here:

1. It's the first sentence. If there are no conclusion indicators, the first sentence is usually the conclusion.
2. "Not necessarily". Any statement of probability, or showing that something might not be the case, is often the conclusion.
3. What receives support? The second and third sentences support the idea that the heavier can may not contain more food.

A. CORRECT. This is the first sentence, which receives support from the other two sentences.

B. This is evidence that supports the idea that a can might be heavier because of water and not because of food.

C. This is evidence that suggests that some cans may be heavier simply because of water weight.

D. Technically, the argument doesn't even say this is true. The final sentence merely says it's *possible* to include more water. The argument doesn't say companies actually *do* include more water. Maybe all companies are scrupulous.

E. The real conclusion is that a heavier can may not have more food. Having more water merely *supports* the idea that a can has less food.

Question 13

QUESTION TYPE: Principle

FACTS:

1. Some three years olds who could count could not remember their own phone numbers.
2. The children did manage to remember their phone numbers once they were taught a song containing their phone numbers.

ANALYSIS: Remember, you are looking for a principle illustrated by the situation. So the stimulus is an example, and the right answer has a principle that matches.

You are not trying to support the stimulus, and you're not trying to figure out what could be true based on the stimulus. You want the stimulus to be an example illustrating the right answer.

All we know here is that songs seem to be useful.

A. Tempting, but there might have been *other* ways the children could have learned. For instance, a nursery rhyme.
B. The children knew the words to express numbers. They just couldn't *remember* their phone numbers.
C. This goes too far. The situation doesn't show that the songs were the *best* method; the children didn't try any other methods beyond those they came up with on their own. We just know songs were useful.
D. We have no idea how the children learned to count. And we have no indication that the children don't know the meaning of numbers.
E. **CORRECT.** This is all we can say. Songs appear to have helped. We don't know if songs are the best method, or the only method, but they helped.

Question 14

QUESTION TYPE: Sufficient Assumption

CONCLUSION: The theorists are wrong, critics shouldn't strive to be value neutral.

REASONING: Critics can never achieve the goal of being value neutral.

ANALYSIS: Here's a quote I read once:

"Why not aim for the stars? You may not reach them, but you probably won't come up with a handful of mud either."

Many of the goals we pursue are unattainable, yet it still makes sense to pursue them, because we move in the right direction.

For instance, you want a 180. Frankly, I doubt you'll get a 180 (*I* didn't get 180). So according to these theorists, you should just give up, it's pointless.

Fuck those guys, right? Who cares that you won't attain the goal of 180. If you improve 10-20 points in the attempt, then the attempt was very worthwhile!

In other words, it may be useful to *attempt* to be value neutral, even if we can never become 100% value neutral. Since we want to prove the theorists correct, we should eliminate this possibility and say that goals are worthless if they can't be achieved.

A. We're trying to prove that critics *shouldn't* try to produce value neutral criticism.
B. **CORRECT.** It *is* impossible to be 100% value neutral, so this answer tells us not to try.
C. This shows a way that critics might fail to be neutral. But this doesn't prove that critics shouldn't *try* to be neutral.
D. The stimulus is talking about what *critics* should do. Readers are only mentioned to describe a benefit of being value neutral. The argument is not about readers!
Also, it's not clear how readers will be affected if critics don't attempt to be value neutral.
E. This weakens the argument by showing that it can be useful to try to avoid value judgments.

Question 15

QUESTION TYPE: Flawed Parallel Reasoning

CONCLUSION: All microscopic organisms must be able to feel pain.

REASONING: Amoeba withdraw from harmful stimuli. Humans do this, and we feel pain.

ANALYSIS: There are two errors here:

1. Humans withdraw because we feel pain. But amoeba might withdraw for a different reason. (Maybe they have an instinct to avoid harm)
2. The conclusion generalizes from amoebas to all microscopic organisms.

Drawings would be distracting and wouldn't make the question any clearer. Do not draw diagrams unless there's a reason. I've seen people get so focussed on unhelpful drawings that they forget to look for the flaws. The two flaws are **1.** forgetting that reasons can differ, and **2.** overgeneralization.

A. **CORRECT.** This generalizes from poets to artists. And it ignores the possibility that there are many reasons for using odd language. People under hypnosis may do so because they have low inhibitions, but poets might have other reasons.
B. This answer doesn't overgeneralize (e.g. from corporations to all businesses), and it doesn't say that corporations *definitely* act the same as non-profits. (The conclusion says "probably").
C. This doesn't overgeneralize from one type of athlete to all athletes. And the rest of the argument isn't terrible. We know "most" athletes have the same reason for practice. Since all boxers practice to excel, it does seem "probable" skaters have the same reason. Probable = most.
D. This is a good argument. The second sentence is completely irrelevant. But the first sentence does prove the third sentence. Generally and probably are both synonyms for "most". So if predatory birds "generally" hunt alone, then it does seem "probable" that a given type of predatory bird (hawks) hunts alone.
E. This answer is part right because it says that the reason for something is similar (though not the same) in two different cases. But it doesn't overgeneralize to *all* mountains.

Question 16

QUESTION TYPE: Strengthen - Exception

CONCLUSION: Sunspots probably help cause changes in hare populations.

REASONING: Sunspots are correlated with changes in hare populations.

ANALYSIS: This is an open ended argument. There are a million reasons why sunspots could affect hare populations. You're trying to prove that correlation = causation in this case, so you just have to eliminate answers that provide a link.

A. The stimulus says increases in predator populations drive hares to forests and thus lead to shrinking hare populations. And this answer shows that sunspots affect predator populations.
B. **CORRECT.** This says that weather affects hare populations, and sunspots *don't* have anything to do with it. So this doesn't strengthen the idea that sunspots are a cause.
C. Hare populations are linked to changes in predators. If predators get more effective due to sunspots, then this will affect hares.
D. You might think this repeats the stimulus, but the LSAT never does that. A correlation just means that when one thing goes up, the other thing also goes up. This answer adds new information: the *amount* of the increase in sunspots and hare populations is also highly correlated. e.g. A 16% increase in sunspots leads not just to an increase in hares, but a ~16% increase.
E. The stimulus says hare populations depend on availability of food – there is less food in forests, and hare populations decline. So if sunspots decrease grass, then it makes sense that hare populations would also decline.

Question 17

QUESTION TYPE: Most Strongly Supported

FACTS:

Successful Economy --> Flourishing Science --> young people excited about science --> good communication

Contrapositive:

~~Good Communication~~ --> ~~Young people excited about science~~ --> ~~flourishing science~~ --> ~~successful economy~~

ANALYSIS: I normally don't draw "most strongly supported" questions, but this one is conditional. All the statements in the stimulus can be connected.

It's important to remember what your diagram means. There is a time element to these statements. A successful economy requires an *active* flourishing community. An active flourishing community requires that *past* young people were once excited. A community might continue to flourish for a while even if current youth are bored with science.

A. This is a mistaken reversal of the final sentence.
B. "Depends principally"? We know excited young people are a necessary condition, but they may not be the main one.
   Something can be a necessary condition without being the *principal* necessary condition.
C. **CORRECT.** This follows from the logical chain I drew in the "Facts" section. A successful economy leads to good communication. That means there was good communication at some point in the past, since that led to past young people getting interested in science and forming the current scientific community.
D. The stimulus only says that "many" youth must *resolve* to become scientists. This answer says "most" youth must *actually* become scientists. That's far stronger. Resolving to do something doesn't mean you'll do it, and many is not most.
E. Nonsense. Good communication was only mentioned as a factor necessary for encouraging youth to want to become scientists. It's possible that an individual scientific *project* can succeed without good communication.

Question 18

QUESTION TYPE: Flawed Reasoning

CONCLUSION: Most businesses that currently don't have videoconferencing would benefit by buying it.

REASONING: Most companies that have bought videoconferencing equipment have benefitted.

ANALYSIS: This argument has a sample bias. It's possible that the businesses that bought videoconferencing equipment *knew* they would benefit from it.

Meanwhile, the businesses that haven't bought it have no use for videoconferencing, so they know they wouldn't benefit.

A. Not quite. The argument said that many businesses actually did benefit from the equipment, so the argument is stronger than this answer choice implies.
   Example of flaw: Many businesses pay for expensive lunches for their managers. So clearly these lunches are worth the cost.
B. This describes a mistaken reversal of a conditional statement. The argument didn't do this. You should *never* pick this type of answer unless you've found a conditional reasoning error in the argument.
   Example of flaw: Video conferencing will help businesses. So anything that isn't video conferencing won't help businesses.
C. This is a different flaw.
   Example of flaw: Johnson said the free money making machine will be useful because he likes the color of the machine. Johnson has made a stupid argument. Therefore it's not a good idea to take the free money making machine.
D. **CORRECT.** See the explanation above. Businesses that bought the equipment probably knew they had a use for it. Meanwhile, businesses that haven't bought it probably realize they *don't* have a use for it.
E. This is a different flaw. The argument didn't compare cost or value.
   Example of flaw: Pizza costs more than water, which is free. So pizza is more useful than water.

53

Question 19

QUESTION TYPE: Necessary Assumption

CONCLUSION: None of the trucks purchased 3 years ago were diesel powered.

REASONING: The company purchased 20 trucks 3 years ago. They sold none of those trucks this year, but they did sell all of their diesel trucks this year.

ANALYSIS: I found this question very difficult, and had to read it three times then come back to it. If the company sold all its diesel trucks last year, how could it not have sold any of the 20 trucks 3-year old if they were diesel powered?

It turns out I made a simple oversight. What if the company sold some of the 20 trucks *last* year, or *two* years ago?

I'll give a numerical example. Let's say the company owned five diesel trucks of type X. Three years ago, they bought four diesel trucks of type D. They also own two regular trucks, type T.

Two years ago, they sell all D trucks. And last year year they sell all their remaining diesel trucks, the X's. Here's the stock of trucks at the end of each year:

Four years ago: XXXXX TT
Three years ago: XXXXX DDD TT
Two years ago: XXXXX DDD TT
Last year: XXXXX TT
This year: TT

So in this example, the company did buy diesel trucks three years ago (DDD). It didn't sell them last year, but only because it already sold them two years ago.

A. Not required.
   Negation: One truck sold last year was gasoline powered, the rest were diesel.
B. Who cares what used trucks the company bought? The stimulus is about the 20 *new* trucks.
   Negation: The company also bought a used truck 3 years ago.
C. It doesn't matter whether the company bought other trucks. We only care about the 20 trucks bought three years ago.
   Negation: Two years ago, the company bought a new gasoline powered truck.
D. CORRECT. If some trucks were sold two years ago, then they could have been diesel trucks even though they weren't sold last year.
   Negation: The company sold some of the 20 trucks earlier than last year.
E. We don't care about trucks purchased *more* than 3 years ago. The question is about trucks purchased *exactly* 3 years ago.
   Negation: The company still has a truck it bought 18 years ago. Wowza!

Question 20

QUESTION TYPE: Flawed Reasoning

CONCLUSION: Telepathy is possible between people who are psychologically close, such as between friends or family.

REASONING: A good friend or family member often knows what you are thinking.

ANALYSIS: This is a tricky question, because it uses the word "psychic" in an uncommon sense. Most people think psychic means "telepathic" or "paranormal". That's definition number one in most dictionaries. But look at definition two from my Oxford dictionary:

Psychic 2. of or relating to the soul or mind: he dulled his psychic pain with gin.

This is really the only sensible definition of "psychic" in the context of the question. If you read "psychic" as meaning paranormal, then the first sentence would mean: "It is indeed possible that psychic people are psychic". That's not just circular reasoning – it's bloody stupid. No one would make such an argument, and the LSAC would never print it. So E, one of the most popular answer choices, is wrong. If there are two possible meanings in an argument, you should avoid the totally ridiculous meaning.

You should ask yourself: why are they telling me this? The author is saying close family members know each other's thoughts, and therefore they must be telepathic. The author's error is ignoring an obvious alternate explanation: family members have experience with each other. They know common reactions and body language.

A. Sample size is not well understood. You can have reliable results from just a few hundred people. And the bigger the effect, the smaller the sample size required. The "amazing" frequency here is presumably so remarkable that only a small sample is needed.
   You do not need a large sample size to determine that arsenic is often fatal if ingested. You *do* need a large sample to conclude that a green button will lead to more website sales than a blue button.
B. **CORRECT.** You're allowed to use common sense on the LSAT (yes, really!). You know from experience that you can often guess what close friends and family are thinking. You're not telepathic – you just know them pretty well.
C. What emotion? This answer didn't happen. **Example of flaw:** You've *got* to work on this business with me! Don't you care about me at all? I'd be so sad if you didn't help.
D. The author didn't say this. They said family members have an "amazing" ability to know what we're thinking. Presumably family knows far more than the norm. But regular people could still sometimes get things right.
E. Very tempting, but this answer depends on a misunderstanding of the full meaning of "psychic". See the explanation above.

Question 21

QUESTION TYPE: Weaken - Exception

CONCLUSION: Sulfur fumes permanently damage your sense of smell.

REASONING: Workers from a sulfur factory identified fewer scents than a control group did.

ANALYSIS: There are a million and one ways to weaken an argument like this. I didn't bother pre-phrasing anything. I just opened my mind to possibilities, eliminated the easy answers, and focussed more narrowly on what was left.

A. **CORRECT.** This would have been a factor for both the factory workers and the control group, so this couldn't really have affected anything. Don't let the term "not perfectly" throw you – this answer is useless. It sounds like the smells were close enough for the study to be useful.
B. This means the sulfur workers were tested in a smelly factory. Maybe they couldn't identify the smells because of the overpowering smells in the factory. It's very reasonable to assume that the sulfur smell could overpower scents. Sulfur smells like rotten egg farts. You can use this kind of knowledge – true facts about the world are warranted assumptions.
C. This shows the control group was experienced at identifying scents. That experience could explain why they identified more scents.
D. Maybe the other noxious fumes cause loss of one's sense of smell.
E. This is like answer C. The factory workers don't know as many smells, so it's unreasonable to expect them to identify as many smells as the control group did.

Question 22

QUESTION TYPE: Principle

PRINCIPLE:

2+ Overdue AND Children's Books AND Previous Fine --> Fine

APPLICATION: Kessler has more than one book overdue.

ANALYSIS: This is a straightforward conditional reasoning question. There are *three* sufficient conditions to establish that we must fine someone:

1. At least one of the overdue books is not a children's book
2. The person has a previous fine
3. More than one book overdue

Kessler meets the third condition. The stimulus says we must "justify" the application of the principle. So we need all three conditions. The right answer must show that Kessler meets the other two.

A. I almost chose this. But, the second condition is that one of the *overdue books* is not a children's book. This answer just says that Kessler has *some* books out that aren't children's books. Maybe all his *overdue* books are children's books.
B. **CORRECT.** This meets both missing conditions.
   1. One of the overdue books isn't for children
   2. Kessler has been fined before.
   Since the application contained the other sufficient condition, this answer proves the necessary condition.
C. The first condition works. Since Kessler does have some books out on loan that are overdue, this answer proves they must be non-children's. But the second condition doesn't work. We need to know that Kessler was fined previously, not just that he previously had overdue books.
D. This meets the second condition: Kessler was fined before. But this fails the first condition. We need to know that Kessler has some overdue books that aren't children's books.
   The final bit is fluff that adds nothing ("none of the fines were for children's books")
E. We need to know that Kessler *was* fined, but this answer says that he wasn't.

Question 23

QUESTION TYPE: Most Strongly Supported

FACTS:

1. Most medical lawsuits happen because people think their doctors are negligent or careless.
2. Doctors are less compassionate than they used to be, and more rude and patronizing.
3. This is because doctors view medicine as a science, and because certain economic incentives encourage doctors to treat patients rudely.

ANALYSIS: On most strongly supported questions you need to see how the facts fit together. I've rearranged the facts from the stimulus into three key groupings. I prephrased the answer as "economic incentives and the view of medicine as a science contribute to lawsuits", but the right answer didn't do this.

Instead the right answer just rephrased the second sentence of the stimulus (note: not the second fact above.)

A. We know that economic incentives are a factor. But that doesn't mean they are the main cause. For instance, we also know that the view that medicine is a science encourages lawsuits.
B. We know that both economic incentives and the view of medicine as a science encourage doctors to treat patients rudely. But we don't know why doctors view medicine as a science – the stimulus didn't say. You can't say that two things are linked just because they produce the same effect.
C. Careful. We know that most lawsuits arise due to patients' perceptions. But perceptions can be accurate! So perceived negligence could be actual negligence, and the lawsuits could be justified.
D. This is way too strong. The scientific outlook certainly has some downsides (rudeness, etc.), but it may have advantages as well.
E. **CORRECT.** This is just a restatement of the second sentence. Doctors view medicine as a science, and this makes them less compassionate. The way you view something is an action, and being less compassionate is the same as not caring.

Question 24

QUESTION TYPE: Parallel Reasoning

CONCLUSION: Even settling --> poured while ground was dry OR crack

REASONING: Wet --> ~~Solid Foundation~~ --> ~~Settle Evenly~~ or Crack

ANALYSIS: I solved this question in 20 seconds. I just looked at the structure of the conclusion, which said "either A or B will be true". Only one answer, A, matched that structure.

That's the easy way, and probably how you should solve a question like this under timed conditions. But, if you're really interested in the structure of arguments, you can follow along with the rest of this explanation to see how this is a good argument, and why the conclusion is true.

Get a pencil and paper and draw it yourself, this is easily the least intuitive argument I've found in logical reasoning, ever. What follows is only for advanced students.

Let's review the logic. The stimulus gives two conditional statements. They join on "not having a settled foundation." I'm drawing the diagram with acronyms, look at the reasoning section above if you're not sure what they refer to:

W --> ~~SF~~ --> SE or C

SE and ~~C~~ --> SF --> ~~W~~

I've drawn the contrapositive as well.

Now, the question does something with logic that I've never seen any other LSAT question do. The conclusion is a correct deduction, but if you read the diagram left to right, you won't see it. Let's take a look at why the deduction is nonetheless true.

Look at the contrapositive diagram. There are two sufficient conditions: settling evenly, and not cracking. We need both to prove the necessary.

(question continued on next page)

If the concrete settles evenly, there are two possibilities: either the concrete cracks, or it doesn't:

SE and C̶ --> SF --> W̶

If the concrete doesn't crack, then we can conclude SF and W̶. (Not wet is the same as dry. There's no in between with wet and dry.)

If the concrete does crack....well, that was the conclusion, right? Either the foundation is dry or it will crack. Voila.

So the two possibilities in the conclusion just describe the concrete either cracking or not cracking.

A. **CORRECT.** This conclusion matches the "either/or" structure from the stimulus. That's really all you need to know, since every other answer fails this test.
   That said, here is the diagram that shows this really matches the structure of the stimulus:

   B̶ and D̶ --> PE --> WP

   Not Blurred is the same as poured evenly in the stimulus, and the two exclusive possibilities are either dark or not dark, which proves the conclusion "dark or working properly". See the analysis above for the full explanation.
B. This says "*both* properly exposed and properly developed". We're looking for something that says either/or.
C. This says "the camera *is* working properly". We're looking for something that says either/or.
D. This says "the photograph *will not be* dark." We're looking for something that says either/or.
E. This says "A or B --> Will not work properly". We're looking for something that says "A --> either B or C".

   Author's note: Here's how I really approach parallel answers: I look to see if the conclusion matches the structure of the conclusion in the stimulus. The harder the argument, the more likely LSAC left you a shortcut by allowing you to quickly eliminate wrong answers for structural reasons. If I still have two answers after looking at structure, then I focus more narrowly, but often only one answer is left.

QUESTION TYPE: Strengthen

CONCLUSION: Evidence indicates that a certain property development hasn't hurt wildlife.

REASONING: Wildlife numbers have increased, and the park can support them.

ANALYSIS: This argument sound pretty good, so you have to ask yourself: "How could this evidence not lead to this conclusion?" Imagining an actual wildlife reserve. What would you look for in a successful reserve? You'd probably want to see lots of animals, and *many different types of species*.

The stimulus only mentions the number of animals increased. What if the development has killed off some species? Maybe the park is now only full of animals that thrive near humans, such as raccoons, squirrels and pigeons. Eww. You can strengthen the argument by eliminating this possibility.

It's perfectly ok to use outside knowledge this way. We're just using it to form guesses. The wrong way to use outside knowledge is to assume something *has* to be true. But thinking something *might* be true lets you answer many questions quickly.

A. **CORRECT.** This shows that species diversity hasn't declined. If all the animals were raccoons, then the argument would not be persuasive. This answer eliminates that possibility.
B. It's not clear how this affects the argument. If the previous survey was also taken in summer, then this has no effect. If the previous survey was taken in another season, then the argument is slightly *weaker* since the recent survey was biased. (Though the survey measured species numbers. The impact of diversity isn't clear.)
C. The stimulus says the park currently *is* capable of supporting the wildlife it contains, so it doesn't matter that it couldn't have done so a decade ago.
D. This *weakens* the argument. Maybe the old techniques found 10% of animals, and now we found 90%. The "increase" is just a mirage. There could even be fewer animals.
E. The conclusion is only about how animal life is doing. Plants are nice, but they don't matter here.

Question 26

QUESTION TYPE: Paradox

PARADOX: Life spans have increased, and we are healthier. Yet we have a higher rate of serious infections.

ANALYSIS: We need something that explains why infections are up even though health in general has improved. Answer E does this by showing that our health treatments only work because they expose people to infections. (e.g. chemotherapy)

Most people get this question wrong. It's a very good question, because it tests your ability to spot detail. The stimulus says that the *rate* of infections has increased. An example of rate is "37 infections per thousand people". Answer choice D is the most popular answer, but it says *number* of infections. An example of a number is "37".

People confuse number and rate all the time. Take crime statistics. Cities tend to be *safer* than rural regions. New York city has a high *number* of murders, because millions of people live there. But the murder *rate* in NYC is actually quite low.

A. You must take "some" at its weakest on answer choices. This answer could mean that 0.00001% of doctors prescribe the wrong medicine. That doesn't affect anything.
B. This doesn't explain anything about infections.
C. This doesn't explain why infections have increased, even though health is better.
D. This is incredibly tempting. It is warranted to assume that population has increased – everyone knows this is true. So based on this answer, we can say that there is a higher *number* of serious infections.
   But the stimulus is talking about *rate,* not number! Rate = amount of infections per capita. So the total population has nothing to do with the rate.
E. **CORRECT.** This shows that the treatments that improve our health also increase the infection rate.

Section IV - Reading Comprehension
Passage 1 - The Washington Color School
Questions 1-6

Paragraph Summaries

1. Sam Gilliam was part of the Washington Color School, a group of abstract African-American painters.
2. Gilliam thought African-American art was too conservative and too overtly political. He wanted art that abstractly expressed the African-American experience.
3. Gilliam captured the African-American experience with folded drapes.

Analysis

I normally don't teach LSAT vocabulary words, but this passage uses one that crops up often enough that you should know it: representational.

Representational art is the opposite of abstract art. And the word itself contains the key to its definition: representation.

You've been to art galleries. You've seen abstract art, and representational art, you just didn't necessarily know the word for the latter. Any picture you saw that painted a real object from the world is "representational", meaning that a painting of a fruit bowl "represents" the fruit bowl.

Rene Magritte played with this idea in 1928, when he painted "The Treachery Of Images". It shows a pipe, with the text "this is not a pipe". The painting is, in fact, not a pipe. It is merely a representation of a pipe.

A purely abstract painting, on the other hand, does *not* represent anything. Think of Jackson Pollack's work, or google "Voice of Fire", a work whose purchase caused no little controversy in Canada.

If you're clear on representational vs. abstract, then you will find some reading comprehension passages and logical reasoning questions easier to understand.

This passage is a good example. The first paragraph confuses many students. But all it's really saying is that the Washington Color School was more abstract than preceding groups.

Likewise, look at the start of the second paragraph. Gilliam rejected the strictly representational and explicitly political art of his African-American contemporaries.

It's easy to read over that sentence and not understand what it's talking about. But the passage will make more sense if you think of what such a painting would look like.

"The Problem We All Live With" by Norman Rockwell is an example of such a piece. Rockwell was not African-American (as a Canadian, I confess ignorance of African-American political art of the 1960s), but his painting is both strictly a representation of a scene, and explicitly political in that Rockwell criticized the crowds who taunted the young girl as she was escorted to school.

Gilliam thought paintings like that were too conservative. He wanted to represent the African-American experience through purely abstract works. Now, I'm not enough of an art connoisseur to understand how abstract works can represent an experience, but you don't need to know that. If you understand everything I've written so far than you know more than most students do when they read this passage.

The final paragraph describes how Gilliam aimed to achieve his effects. I still frankly don't know enough to say how draped canvasses represented the African-American experience, but that's not something you need to know. For a paragraph like the third one, you just need to be able to quote details if a question asks about them.

Question 1

DISCUSSION: Main point and primary purpose questions are much the same: use your paragraph summaries, and ask yourself "why is the author telling me this?"

This passage is a description of Gilliam's work, of its context within the African-American abstract art movement, and of what Gilliam was trying to achieve.

A. **CORRECT.** This is the best fit. This passage is above all a description of Gilliam's work.
B. Gilliam's work was far more than political. See lines 30-34. Gilliam wanted to describe the whole of human experience.
C. The passage mentions Gilliam's style, but not the *evolution* of Gilliam's style.
D. The passage does say that Gilliam's views were rare (line 35). But that's not the *point* of the passage, and the passage doesn't do much to *prove* that Gilliam's views were rare. This answer choice describes an argument devoted to *proving* that few others held Gilliam's views.
E. The passage didn't describe any technical limitations.

Question 2

DISCUSSION: Gilliam's work was abstract, yet also represented the human experience.

Representational art is any art that shows recognizable objects, such as people, animals, photographs, etc. Gilliam's art was abstract, not representational.

See the analysis section for a longer description of what representational art is.

A. This painting is representational, because it shows a man. Gilliam's work was abstract.
B. This art is still somewhat representational, because it shows photographs. Gilliam's work was abstract and represented no forms.
C. Same as A and B: this answer describes representational art. Gilliam's art was abstract.
D. This has canvas, like Gilliam's work, but this art is representational, because it shows the sea and clouds.
E. **CORRECT.** This is the only answer that describes abstract art. There are no recognizable forms in this piece. Also, this answer matches lines 39-41: Gilliam folded canvases onto each other.

Question 3

DISCUSSION: Lines 27 explains why the author mentioned the collage artist. Gilliam did not much like that type of art. "Though" is a logical word that indicates opinion; it's important to note any lines that start with though, but, however, etc.

So the collage art was an example of the popular art that Gilliam rejected as overly conventional.

A. Gilliam was *part of* the Washington Color School. The Color School made abstract art. The collage art was representational, not abstract.
B. We don't even know if there *was* animosity between abstract and representational artists, in general. We only know Gilliam didn't think much of abstract art.
C. This might be true, but it's not the point. The only reason the author mentions a collage is to give us an idea of what Gilliam objected to. The passage does not focus on the popularity of art, only line 27 mentions it, in passing.
D. **CORRECT.** Lines 27-35 make this clear. Lines 21-27 explain the collage, lines 27-29 explain Gilliam's reasoning for disliking it, and lines 29-35 show Gilliam's alternate approach.
   There's nothing particularly special about the collage. The passage mentioned it because it's always nice to have an example for clarity.
E. Gilliam's art was *not* concerned primarily with political issues. Gilliam wanted to represent all of human experience. See lines 29-35.

Question 4

DISCUSSION: We can see Gilliam's opinions in two places: lines 16-21 and 28-30. Gilliam clearly is dissatisfied with representational art, but he is not too harsh about it.

A. This is exceptionally strong answer. If Gilliam felt this way, he would basically spit on the art of those who made representational art.
   Gilliam clearly dislikes representational art, but he hasn't expressed open hatred.
B. **CORRECT.** The passage is clear about this. See lines 16-21, and 28-30.
C. "Whimsical" means means playfully or fancifully. Gilliam seems deadly serious about art.
   If you don't know a word, see if it reminds you of similar words, such as "whimsy" or "whim".
   Acting on a whim is probably a phrase you know.
D. Lines 16-21 and 28-30 clearly show that Gilliam disapproves of representational art.
E. Lines 16-21 and 28-30 contradict this answer.

Question 5

DISCUSSION: There's no fast way to answer this type of question. Either you remember the details mentioned in the answer choices, or you don't.

I personally check each answer against the passage. Because I have a good method for retaining where information is located, this takes me 2-10 seconds per answer, and is much faster than staring at the answers and going "hmm....." while trying to think my way to disproving them.

A. Lines 45-49 say this.
B. Lines 35-39 say this.
C. Lines 34-35 say this.
D. Lines 12-21 show this. You don't need to find the specific lines to disprove it. If you know that Gilliam was part of the Washington Color School, then you should know that the Color School was different from Gilliam's contemporaries. Gilliam rejected the style of his contemporaries.
E. **CORRECT.** The passage never mentions inspiration in general. Lines 43-45 mention that laundry "partially" inspired Gilliam, but we have no evidence that ordinary images are always the most inspirational images.

Question 6

DISCUSSION: A is the most common wrong answer on this question. I think it's tempting because it feels similar to Gilliam's attitude of defiance towards representational art.

But the similarities end there. On "author agrees" questions, you must interpret the statements literally. Interpreted literally, A is insane. Completely bonkers. I've seen few more insane statements on the LSAT.

No one would *ever* believe A. Not even that guy that made "Artist's Shit".

A. This statement is crazy.
   You must take LSAT statements literally. Interpreted literally, this statement is batshit insane. For example, it would include "You should not worry if your painting is so aesthetically ugly that it literally frightens people to death". No one believes that, including Gilliam.
B. Gilliam's art is abstract, so it's unlikely he believes this.
C. Lines 36-39 contradict this.
D. **CORRECT.** Lines 30-34 show that Gilliam was concerned with showing the complexity of human experience. And the first paragraph shows that Gilliam was part of the Washington Color Field school, so presumably he liked their philosophy.
E. Lines 36-39 show that Gilliam cared little for public expectations.

Passage 2 - Multiplayer Online Games (Comparative)
Questions 7-13

Paragraph Summaries

Passage A
1. Description of online multiplayer games.
2. Edward Castronova notices that games have economies.
3. Castronova realized that players auction video game goods on online auction sites.
4. Video game players are creating real world wealth.

Passage B
1. Most games ban players from trading game items for money.
2. Questions about taxation of video game goods.
3. In-game only wealth should be treated like gathering fish: taxed only upon sale.
4. We should tax the sale of items earned in game. This prevents virtual tax shelters and is in line with tax policy.

Analysis

These two passages are completely different in tone, yet many students do not notice the difference. If you struggle with tone and author's opinion questions, you should go over these passages with a fine toothed comb. Look for every word that indicates emotion or value judgement.

The first passage has a tone of excited discovery. Wow, look! There's an economy here. This is so cool guys! Oh my god, they're selling things! For money! Wooooo, economics!!

I'm exaggerating, but this passage is about as enthusiastic as LSAT reading comprehension passages will get. Take a look at lines 17-20:
"....Castronova *stared*.....he realized with a *shock* what he was looking at."

Emphasis mine. I've never seen the LSAT describe someone as shocked, or experiencing any extreme emotion. This passage is astonishingly high on the LSAT emotional scale.

Notice that Castronova's article was published in 2004. I was at university in 2004. We had desktop computers, and no one had cellphones. I think I had gotten a high speed internet connection six years prior.

So, massive online games were *very* new. This article reflects that newness. An economist was only just noticing that these games have economies, and he wasn't looking for economies within the games. It was a surprise discovery.

The tone of passage B is very different. This article was published in 2007. The world has had three years to catch up to the fact that games have economies. Now the legal system has taken notice of online games. This paper discusses how to tax online game assets.

Tax policy? Bleh, so dull. In 2004 players would have been shocked that the government would take an interest in their games. But now (2014 at the time of writing) it's obvious that game earnings have real value, and passage B reflects an early version of this understanding.

As for the content of passage B, the argument seems rather sensible. The author argues for a clean division between games as entertainment and games as centers of e-commerce.

This passage is interesting in that five out of seven questions are entirely based on the main point of each passage and the relationship between them. One question (number 8) is partially based on this, and only question 13 is based on specific details.

On every passage, you should ask yourself "why are they telling me this". It's a useful question everywhere. But on these passages, it's essential.

Question 7

DISCUSSION: The first passage is about Edward Castronova's excited discovery of real economies in online games. The second passage is about how we should *not* tax online games, for the most part.

A. The first passage is about Edward Castronova's *discovery*, not about the economist himself. And the second passage is about taxation, not intellectual property.
B. **CORRECT.** This matches both passages. Read my analysis section on the previous page if you're not sure why this is the answer.
C. The first passage doesn't mention the *growth* of online games. And the second title is too broad: the second passage is only about taxation, not all law.
D. The first passage is definitely not a guide to making money by playing games. And the second passage is about how to tax *video games,* not how to deal with online tax shelters in general.
E. These titles are too strong. *Communism* was a new economic paradigm. Online games are just a small niche in the economy. And passage B is mainly about *not* collecting revenue from video games.

Question 8

DISCUSSION: Virtual players skin animals to create valuable items. This generates wealth (lines 23-25). Real life fisherman gather fish, which produces a good which can be eaten or sold.

So both activities generate wealth using labour. One is virtual, one is real. The second passage suggests that such activities should not be taxed unless and until the good is sold. (lines 45-51)

A. "The latter" is fishing. Lines 45-51 say that fish is "property". By any normal definition of the word, property is a form of wealth.
B. **CORRECT.** Read lines 45-51 for the full picture. The author only mentions fishing because it is similar to generating wealth online. (Lines 23-25 say that skinning animals online creates wealth.)
C. Lines 50-51 say that creating wealth online should *not* be taxed.
D. The author thinks *neither* gathering fish nor generating wealth online should be taxed. (lines 45-51)
E. The fishing in line 49 is real world fishing.

Question 9

DISCUSSION: See the passage analysis section for a full overview of the two passages. The author of passage A is very excited about the discovery of the new online video game economy. Lines 17-18 describe Edward Castronova's shock at finding an economy. This is strong language for the LSAT. The author of passage A is excited.

Passage B has a scholarly tone. See lines 44-45: "This article will argue that....policy support that result."

———————

A. Neither passage is critical or apprehensive (afraid of) the online video game economy.
B. The *second* passage is academic. This question asks about the style of the first passage. And neither passage is dismissive.
C. **CORRECT.** See lines 7-8 "curious", or 13 "even more interesting" or 17-18 "stared....with a shock". The author of passage A is extremely excited about this new discovery.
D. Passage A is definitely curious about this new phenomenon. Undecided is not the right word however. Here's an example of an undecided but curious article:
   "I don't know about these online games. They seem difficult. Can you really make money in them? That's so different from anything I know. Is it really possible? I bet there's some mistake here. I definitely want to know more though."
E. Passage A is definitely enthusiastic. They are not skeptical however. No part of the passage questions whether Castronova is correct.

Question 10

DISCUSSION: This question tests the same thing as question 7: did you understand the differences in tone between the two passages?

Passage A is excited about a new phenomenon. Passage B is a scholarly discussion of how to apply the law to this somewhat less new phenomenon.

You can use the scholarly element in passage B to eliminate wrong answers. Only answers A and D have a scholarly second title.

———————

A. This answer's title for the first article sounds scholarly. The tone of passage A is more like "woah, there's artificial intelligence here!".
B. Both of these titles describe newspaper stories. But the second passage was scholarly. Also, the first title should be "Retailers discover e-commerce" and the second should be "how the law applies to e-commerce"
C. The first part is pretty good. The second title is not good however. It describes a newspaper article about a debate between scientists.
D. **CORRECT.** The first title has the same tone of discovery. The second title has the same tone of scholarly discussion of how to apply the law to a new area.
E. Edward Castronova is notable because he noticed the new online economy. He isn't a renegade. And the second title describes a newspaper article, not a scholarly article.

Question 11

DISCUSSION: The first passage seems general. You don't need to understand any economics or video game concepts to follow along.

The second passage is scholarly, and probably came from a journal.

Some of the wrong answers are goofy. Clearly, neither passage was from a science fiction novel or a speech before a legislature.

_____

A. CORRECT. If you don't see that this is correct, reread my analysis section and then reread the passage. Look for any words that indicate tone or style.

B. I studied economics. A technical journal for economists would probably sound like this: "Does the marginal utility of online video games justify the opportunity cost of playing them? And can rents created within the game provide an alternate and complementary incentive for participation?"

C. Science fiction novel? Passage A is talking about the real world.

D. Passage *B* is from a law journal. Passage A is probably from a generalist magazine. And neither article is from a speech to a legislature.

E. If you chose this, I'm not even sure you read the passage. This answer is just silly: who would read a science-fiction novel that discussed video game tax policy at length?

Question 12

DISCUSSION: Another question about the relationship between the passages. Knowing the main point of each passage would answer at least three questions on this passage.

Passage A describes a new phenomenon. Passage B describes how to deal with the taxation issues that arise from that new phenomenon.

_____

A. CORRECT. The first part is obviously correct. You may have hesitated about the second part. Are online game economies really a problem? Yes. See lines 56-58. If we don't tax online economies to some extent, they will be a tax shelter.

To be clear: "A problem raised" is not really a negative term. The author of passage B could think "online economies are excellent. There's just one small problem (issue) we have to address".

B. Passage A isn't describing an economic theory. The passage just describes Edward Castronova's discovery of online economies, in an article addressed at the general public. A theory would be like "online economies behave exactly like real world economies. This paper will show...."

C. Passage B didn't say it would be *difficult* to tax online games. Passage B was debating *whether* and *how* we should tax online games.

D. Hogwash. Before Passage A, there wasn't even a common interpretation of online economies. Edward Castronova discovered them. So there's no common interpretation for Passage B to affirm.

E. Passage B isn't theoretical. An article is not theoretical just because it is scholarly. Passage B is discussing the very *practical* issue of whether we ought to tax online economies.

Question 13

DISCUSSION: This is the trickiest question. Lines 52-55 make a distinction between games that are intentionally commodified, and those that aren't.

The first paragraph of Passage B also makes this distinction, though it's less clear. Paragraph one says "but some actually encourage *it*."

"It" is real world trade in virtual items. It's reasonable to say that those games have been commodified. In game transactions are explicitly viewed as economic transactions by the games' creators.

The creators economize the games by giving intellectual property rights, which is answer D.

A. CORRECT. Lines 52-54 talk about selling *virtual* items for real currency. This answer talks about selling a *real* item for virtual currency. E.g. "I'll sell you my house for $10,000 elf-dollars". This answer would have been correct if it had used the right words, but it used the wrong words instead.

B. The word "avatar" doesn't appear in passage B. This answer has no support.

C. Passage B doesn't mention whether all players gain wealth simply by playing longer. Some games may have high costs that reduce wealth.

D. CORRECT. Lines 26-29 support this. The games that grant intellectual property rights are encouraging real world commerce. This amounts to "intentional commodification".

E. Passage B never mentions whether you can trade elf-dollars for orc-dollars (for example). In fact, passage B doesn't even mention whether you can trade virtual currency for real currency. Passage B only mentions virtual *items* for real currency.

Passage 3 - Success and Talent
Questions 14-19

Paragraph Summaries

1. Opposing view: Some people think that talent is innate.
2. Recent studies suggest that talent only occurs within specific fields of expertise. E.g. Athletes have good reaction time in their sports, but not necessarily in general.
3. Most high performers only became good through training. Even anatomical characteristics can be trained.
4. Motivation is more likely than talent to be a predictor of great ability.

Analysis

This passage is an argument. It's important for you to understand why the author says the things they say.

Their overall point is this: talent is acquired, not innate. The paragraph summaries above show how each section fits into the argument.

The particular details used to support the argument are not that important. You should know where to find details, but you don't need to memorize them. These are the important facts you should retain:

- Talent can be learned
- Top performers largely don't rely on genetic talent
- Motivation and time are required for success
- Some innate talent is required (lines 55-56)

The passage is nuanced. The author does not say their theory is definitely right. Lines 62-64 just say that motivation is "more likely" to be important than innate talent.

And talent is a factor. Height, for example (45-47) definitely matters and can't be changed. And lines 41-45 imply that some innate skills are useful for chess. They're just not essential. If you lack certain innate talents, you can overcome them by training other skills.

Question 14

DISCUSSION: The passage is nuanced. Research suggests that motivation is more likely to be important than innate talent. (lines 62-64)

The author does *not* say that innate talent is useless. For instance, lines 41-45 show that superior innate capacities can help chess players, *but* chess players can overcome these limits with training.

And lines 55-56 show that you need *some* talent to succeed. The author's point is merely that it's not as important as we think.

A. The passage said many traits, such as perception, are *not* inborn. They can be altered by training. The passage did not say that inborn traits (such as height) can be altered by training.
B. The author didn't say that anyone can achieve exceptional levels of performance. Exceptional performance is, by definition, rare. You don't need innate talent for exceptional performance, but there may be other necessary conditions.
C. This goes too far. Lines 41-45 show that superior traits can be useful. Chess players can *circumvent* innate limits with training, but not having innate skill is still somewhat of a disadvantage.
D. **CORRECT.** This is the best summary of the passage. It is appropriately nuanced. The author did not say that their argument is conclusively correct. Lines 62-64 just say that superior performance is "more likely" due to motivation than innate talent.
E. This isn't necessarily true. The psychologists are only mentioned in the first paragraph. The author has presented good evidence that the psychologists are wrong. But that doesn't mean the psychologists will change their beliefs: people often hold onto wrong beliefs.

69

Question 15

DISCUSSION: The final paragraph is the conclusion – line 51 says "therefore". This paragraphs sums up the argument that learned skills are more important than innate talent.

The paragraphs ends by saying that since motivation is required for skills, then motivation is likely more important than talent.

A. What? The final paragraph doesn't even mention education. You can learn skills outside of the education system.
B. There's no contradiction in the final paragraph. I have no idea what this answer choice might refer to.
C. There are two problems here. Recapitulating evidence would mean listing everything that was said in paragraphs two and three. The fourth paragraph simply didn't do this. The fourth paragraph restated the conclusion, but it did not restate the evidence. Restating the evidence would be: "Because studies show that talent is specific to the field of expertise (paragraph 2) and because adult performers were not exceptional as children (paragraph 3)" etc.
The second half of this answer is also false. The fourth paragraph does not discuss future research. Look all you want, you won't find it. Instead, the second paragraph makes a conclusion about the importance of motivation.
D. What possible objection? I have no idea how to disprove this answer. It simply has no basis in paragraph 4.
E. **CORRECT.** The two inferences are:
1. Extended training + a common level of talent may account for outstanding performance.
2. Motivation may be more important than talent.

"Suggests instead" (line 54) is what shows that these *are* inferences. This answer is very abstract. If you see an abstract answer, don't glaze over. There are good odds it's actually the answer. Take the time to figure out what it refers to.

Question 16

DISCUSSION: You must take LSAT answers literally. If a statements says "talent plays no role" then this means talent has *zero* impact. That's a silly idea, and the authors don't agree. Lines 55-57 show that some talent is required.

Yet answer E is the most common answer chosen: it says talent plays *no* role. That's insane.

A. **CORRECT.** I had a bit of difficulty choosing this answer. It feels right, but there's no line in the passage that proves it. Nonetheless, I believe it's well supported.
Consider an adult chess player. They have exceptional memory and perception. Lines 51-55 show that extensive training + reasonable talent is enough for exceptional skill. But the argument doesn't rule out exceptional talent + moderate practice as a way to gain skills.
So does this chess player have exceptional innate talent? We don't know. How would we know? We can see the chess player is skilled. It would be difficult to reconstruct the past and see if these skills were innate or learned.
B. Lines 55-57 contradict this. You don't need the highest level of talent to succeed. You just need the level of talent common to reasonably competent performers.
C. The passage didn't say whether any fields actually do require exceptional talent. And the whole point of the argument is that exceptional talent tends not to be required.
D. This isn't supported. Lines 62-64 say motivation is required, but the passage doesn't say what affects motivation.
E. This answer directly contradicts the passage. Lines 51-57 say that "that level of talent common to all reasonably competent performers" is necessary for exceptional performance. The passage says talent is not as important as we think, but the passage definitely says some talent is necessary.

Question 17

DISCUSSION: This question stem is very clear: it tells you that the passage *literally* says the answer. If you can find the right line, you can be 100% certain of your answer. This type of question tests your recall, and how well you can skim to find information.

Keeping up intense practice is only mentioned in the final paragraph, so you just have to look there. Note that the question is not asking what's necessary for success. The question is asking what's necessary to keep up practice.

It's hard to know what to say about the wrong answers except that they're not mentioned in the passage, or not mentioned as being necessary for practice. The question asks about what's required for practice, not for being skilled.

A. CORRECT. Lines 57-59 say this.
B. Emotional support is never mentioned.
C. The passage never mentions whether instruction at a particular level helps people practice. You might have picked this because lines 36-39 say that early practice is crucial for the vast majority of performers. But the question asks about what is necessary for *practice* itself, not for talent.
D. The passage never mentions leisure.
E. The passage never mentions self-discipline or control.

Question 18

DISCUSSION: Lines 21-27 are the key lines for sifting through these answers. The author uses *new* evidence to argue against an old theory.

That one sentence I wrote above disproves all four wrong answers.

A. The author didn't "revise" a theoretical model. The old model was that talent was innate. The author completely rejects this model.
B. Lines 17-27 show that the author's argument is based on *new* research.
C. CORRECT. Lines 17-27 show that the author's argument is based on new research. The "certain views" is the opposing viewpoint in paragraph 1. The particular class of cases can refer to one of two things: exceptional performers, or, perhaps, those exceptional performers that do not depend on innate talent. (Some cases of exceptional performance may depend on innate talent, because some traits are indeed innate, see lines 45-47)
D. The author mentioned the old viewpoints in paragraph 1, but the author didn't mention any "probable objections" to his new theory. Any new objections would have to take into account the evidence the author refers to paragraphs 2-4.
E. The author's theory is not abstract, and the evidence is not old. Lines 21-27 show that the author uses *new* research. And the author's theory of talent is practical: it's based on elite performance in the real world.

Question 19

DISCUSSION: This question refers to lines 32-35. These lines are precise, and they say two things:

- Chess players have good memory for arrangements of chess pieces in typical chess arrangements.
- Chess players do not have good memory for chess pieces in non-typical arrangements.

The passage doesn't say whether chess players have good memories for other things or for other games.

A. This is the most popular wrong answer. Read lines 32-35 carefully: the passage doesn't say anything about other games. We have no idea how well chess players remember things that don't involve chess pieces.
(In case that doesn't convince you: it's possible that these sequences of moves in other games are *also* typical of chess, in which case chess players would remember them)

B. The passage doesn't mention sequences without spatial elements.

C. Lines 32-35 say that chess player can remember chess configurations. It does sound like remembering a whole game is more challenging than remembering a configuration. But this answer is only talking about easy games. We have no evidence that chess masters are incapable of remembering whole games.

D. **CORRECT.** Specifically, lines 32-35 say that chess players do not have a good memory for *non-typical* configurations of chess pieces.

E. Logical analysis simply isn't mentioned in the passage. There is no evidence to support this answer choice.

Passage 4 - The Physics of Mirrors
Questions 20-27

Paragraph Summaries

1. Description of the field-of-sight explanation for mirrors.
2. Some physicists offer a persuasive, but flawed, front-to-back reversal explanation.
3. This front-to-back explanation is persuasive because it seems natural, but we can't trust our senses with mirrors. They are 2-d, but simulate 3-d.
4. Scientists like the front-to-back explanation because they can separate the observer from the event. But in this case there is no event (reflection) without an observer.

Analysis

You don't necessarily need to know details in this passage. For example, I forgot all the details in paragraph 1. I just know that's where the field-of-sight explanation is.

In fact, as I write this explanation, I don't remember any of the details from paragraphs two and three. So what do I know? I took note of the structural elements of the argument. I remember everything I wrote in the paragraph summaries above, and I know what the author is saying. If a question asks about the details, I know where to find them, because I know the organization of the passage.

The author's main point is that mirrors are deceiving. We should explain them in terms of what actually happens (field-of-sight explanation) rather than what makes intuitive sense (front-to-back explanation).

When we look at a mirror, we imagine 3-d objects. In fact, our eyes focus on mirrors as if we were looking at a 3-d scene, rather than a 2-d object (lines 38-41).

But mirrors are not 3-d. They are flat sheets of glass. There is no object inside them which is the reverse of real world objects. Instead, something happens with light (spare me the details, they're in paragraph 1!) which reverses our vision left-to-right, making the image reversed.

Paragraphs 2-4 are devoted to showing that the front-to-back theory of mirrors is wrong. The front-to-back theory is based on our intuitions. When we look into a mirror, it looks like the objects are reversed from front-to-back.

This theory makes sense in terms of how we imagine mirror objects in our heads (our "mental constructs" of mirror objects). But this theory gives a false impression of what happens in the real world. Lines 34-36 say that we take what we see in mirrors and imagine it wrong in our heads.

Many answers talk about mental constructs, so the test-makers assume you will find them confusing. It's a fancy term for "stuff you imagine". We don't see the real world. Light hits our eyes, and our brains turn that into mental images. These images aren't real, and what you see may not be what someone else sees.

However, in most cases, our mental images of the world give us a good idea of what the world is actually like. But in the case of mirrors, our mental constructs are inaccurate. A mirror is just a flat piece of glass. But we see it as a 3-d scene.

The final paragraph explains another reason why the front-to-back theory is popular. Scientists like to separate objects and observers.

This doesn't work with mirrors. If no one looks into a mirror, there is nothing to see. The phenomenon of a reflected object is only there if an observer can see the object.

(continued on next page)

Analysis Continued

Structural words are extremely important on reading comprehension. They let you skip over the details and focus on a few key points. When you review RC passages, highlight structural words to train yourself to process them automatically. Here are some examples:

- however (line 14)
- it is clearly (line 22)
- yet (line 23)
- however (line 27)
- note (line 38)
- In addition to (line 42)
- However (line 48)

This passage has an unusually high number of structural words. That means the questions will test whether you understand the author's purpose. I'm this paragraph after having written explanations for all the questions on this passage, and almost all of the questions test overall comprehension, not details.

Frankly, these questions are easy if you understand the passage, but almost impossible if you don't. In fact, if you still don't understand the passage, then I fear my explanations may be rather difficult to follow, because I have to use words such as "front-to-back explanation", as that is what this passage is about.

I recommend two steps if you found this passage difficult:

1. Reread the passage, and other hard science passages, until they start to make some sense.
2. Go to your local library, and get 20-30 back issues of the economist. Start reading the science sections.

The Economist science section is about three pages long. It's well written, yet not dumbed down, so it matches the style of LSAT reading comprehension science passages.

Question 20

DISCUSSION: Lines 48-51 contain the answer to this question. In the analysis section I mentioned the importance of structural words such as "however". This question is a perfect example: you should take special notice of lines that follow "however", such as lines 48-51.

A. **CORRECT.** See lines 48-51. The two elements are "what mirrors do" and "what happens when we look into mirrors"
B. The author appears to agree with the field-of-sight explanation in paragraph 1. Whether or not this is true, the main point of the passage is to argue against the front-to-back theory.
C. Nonsense. The author didn't say that no other expert could give an explanation of mirrors.
D. It's true that the explanation of mirrors is still subject to debate. But the author's main point is that one side of the debate is wrong.
E. This answer made me laugh. LSAT authors tend to know everything. They have the truth, and they're here to give it to us. The only time an LSAT author would argue an issue is complicated is if some other person argued the issue was simple.

Question 21

DISCUSSION: This question tests two things:

1. Do you remember that the left-to-right explanation is discussed only in the first paragraph.
2. Can you reread the first paragraph and retain the details long enough to spot the right answer?

Don't make this question more complicated than it needs to be. The right answer is directly in the paragraph. The wrong answers are calculated to confuse you. It should only take about 15 seconds to reread the first paragraph – rereading is far faster than reading the first time.

(left-to-right reversal is part of the field-of-sight explanation, in the first paragraph)

A. Front-to-back is the alternate explanation, it is described in paragraphs 2-4. This questions asks about the left-to-right explanation, which is only mentioned in paragraph 1.
B. **CORRECT.** Lines 10-12 say this.
C. Lines 7-10 say that mirrors images depend on the position of the *observer,* but the position of the object isn't mentioned. Size makes no sense: small objects reverse, and big objects don't? You know from experience that size doesn't affect whether a mirror image reverses.
D. There are no two-dimensional objects. There are two dimensional *images,* but not objects. If you ever come across a perfectly two-dimensional object, call a mathematician.
E. Lines 28-31 mention mental constructs. These are only mentioned to explain why the front-to-back theory is persuasive. Mental constructs have nothing to do with the first paragraph and the field-of-sight theory.

Question 22

DISCUSSION: Lines 28-32 mention mental constructs. That sentence starts with "It seems natural because....mental constructs".

To answer this question, you need to read the previous line, to see what "*it* seems natural because" refers to. "It" is a pronoun. Whenever you see one, you must refer to earlier lines so that you know what "it" is. The LSAT uses this pronoun trick time and again.

The previous sentence says that the front-to-back explanation appeals strongly to people. This is because we deal with mental constructs of objects.

So mental constructs help us to understand and accept the front-to-back explanation of mirrors. By the way, "mental construct" just means images you make in your head. Like when you imagine your dog – it's not a real dog, it's just your imagination. But usually it bears some resemblance to your dog.

This question is extraordinarily confusing, and highlights the importance of going back to the passage. If you understand lines 28-32, then this question is easy. If you don't, then you'll waste time bouncing between nonsensical answers. None of the wrong answers make any sense. All of them refer to things that were never mentioned in the passage.

A. There is no top-to-bottom explanation. This answer is total nonsense designed to confuse you.
B. **CORRECT.** Read lines 26-32 in full and you'll see that mental constructs help us understand the front-to-back explanation.
C. This is a nonsense answer. "Complex perceptual observations" does not appear in the passage.
D. I don't even know what this means. I'm assuming you only picked this because you had no idea what any of the answers meant.
  The passage didn't talk about rejecting associations between constructs and perceptions. In fact, the passage says that mirrors are confusing *because* we assume our mental constructs and objects/perceptions are the same.
E. The passage doesn't talk about overemphasizing senses. This is another nonsense answer.

Question 23

DISCUSSION: The front-to-back explanation is the opposing explanation mentioned in paragraphs 2-4.

The author does not accept this theory. Lines 26-28 say that it is successful "to a point". Right away we can narrow things down to D or E.

In the passage analysis section I highlighted words that indicated the author's opinion, such as "however". Those words are crucial to the argument, and to answering this question.

———————————

A. The author only thinks the front-to-back explanation is successful "to a point". See the analysis above.
B. Same as A.
C. Same as A and B.
D. It is not a bad thing to be consistent with previous theories. You may know that from common sense. In any case the author does not say consistency is a bad thing.
E. **CORRECT.** The front-to-back theory does not offer an explanation of mirrors based on the observer. It treats the objects in mirrors as real, which is false (21-25). Lines 48-54 say that any good theory of mirrors must consider what happens when an observer looks in.

Question 24

DISCUSSION: You might think that the point of the passage is to compare two theories of mirrors. But the field-of-sight theory is only mentioned to establish that we have a pretty good explanation of mirrors. After the first paragraph, the field-of-sight theory is not mentioned again.

Instead, the rest of the passage discussed the front-to-back theory. The main point of the passage is that the front-to-back theory is not satisfactory. This is because it doesn't consider what happens when we look into mirrors (lines 48-54).

———————————

A. The passage doesn't give any evidence against the field-of-sight theory. It appears the author agrees that this theory is correct.
B. This is a tempting answer, but the front-to-back theory is *not* based on empirical evidence. We use our mental constructs to imagine the front-to-back theory (lines 28-32), but these constructs are contrary to fact (lines 34-36). The front-to-back explanation is based on a false idea.
C. Lines 48-51 did mention two necessary conditions for an explanation of mirrors, but this is not the same as listing difficulties that need to be overcome. A difficulty is a specific obstacle that needs to be removed, for instance "we need to construct a physically perfect mirror" or "we need to figure out a way to measure light entering a mirror".
D. **CORRECT.** Paragraphs 2-4 are dedicated to showing why the front-to-back theory is inadequate. See the passage analysis section and the discussion above for more details.
E. The passage does explain why the front-to-back theory is accepted. But it is not because of theoretical support. Instead, the front-to-back theory receives support for two reasons:

1. The front-to-back explanation seems natural to us, due to the way we imagine mirrors (lines 26-32)
2. Scientists like to separate the observer from the phenomenon (lines 42-45)

Question 25

DISCUSSION: Author agreement questions are heavily based on the passage. You can usually find a specific line that proves the right answer.

Questions like this show that it's worthwhile to take extra time reading and understanding the passage. This will improve your recall of the details, and help you spot the right answer on this type of question.

A. The author actually never mentions optical equipment or mirror quality. Presumably an explanation for mirrors should make sense even for poorly constructed mirrors, and even if we don't have fancy equipment to confirm the theory.
B. The author only mentioned two theories of mirrors, and they only argued one of them was wrong (the front-to-back) theory. So the author doesn't say why mirrors explanations fail *in general*.
C. **CORRECT.** Lines 42-45 support this. They say that the observer/phenomenon separation is part of the reason why some scientists support the front-to-back theory.
D. Lines 28-30 say "we" think in terms of mental constructs. Mental constructs seem natural. The passage doesn't say any of us avoid mental constructs. And even some scientists like the front-to-back theory, so they must be thinking in terms of mental constructs.
E. This is almost right. If it had ended by saying "mental constructs interfere....with an accurate understanding of how mirrors work" then this answer would have been right.
  But the answer doesn't say that. You need to read every word on the LSAT. The passage doesn't say that mental constructs interfere with our understanding of perceptions.

Question 26

DISCUSSION: The author appears to think that the field-of-sight theory is correct. It's discussed in the first paragraph. If you reread that paragraph, you'll find not one criticism of the theory.

The field-of-sight theory is only mentioned in order to provide a contrast to the front-to-back theory. The author argues that the front-to-back theory is wrong. Presumably the field-of-sight theory does not share any of those errors. Otherwise the author would have said so. From the descriptions of the two theories, they seem very different.

A. The only traditional desire is the one mentioned in lines 42-45: scientists want to separate observer and phenomenon. There's no mention of a traditional desire to simplify explanations.
B. **CORRECT.** Lines 21-25 show that the front-to-back theory is based on the false idea that mirror objects are 3-d. Since the author does *not* say the same thing about the field-of-sight theory, we can assume the field-of-sight theory does not make such an assumption. From the description in paragraph one, the left-to-right reversal in the field-of-sight theory doesn't depend on the belief that the mirror image is 3-d.
C. The *front-to-back* theory does not take into account what an observer sees (see the final paragraph). But this question is talking about the field-of-sight theory.
D. The field-of-sight theory is only mentioned in the first paragraph, and the first paragraph doesn't say that people fail to understand the reality of mirrors.
E. The field-of-sight theory is only mentioned in the first paragraph. The author appears to approve of it. They never say it is incorrect or unsuccessful.

Question 27

DISCUSSION: Read lines 34-41 to get the full picture. We look *at* objects. If you see an apple, you focus on it. But you look *into* landscapes. Think about what you see when you're on top of a hill, overlooking the land below. You look off into the distance, you are not focussed.

A mirror is an object. It's a flat surface. Yet we look *into* it, like we would any landscape. That's pretty amazing. I can't think of any other object that has this affect on us.

So lines 39-40 help illustrate what it means for mirrors to show us 3-d reality.

A. Lines 39-40 are talking about *seeing* objects in a mirror. They don't mention *imagining* objects.
B. Lines 39-40 don't mention mental constructs. This answer is designed to confuse you by mentioning an irrelevant concept from earlier in the passage.
C. CORRECT. See the explanation above. Knowing that we focus *into* mirrors helps us understand how they are like landscapes, not objects.
D. Mental constructs are mentioned in lines 28-30. They aren't relevant here. We when focus our eyes on the distance, that's a physical act in the real world, and not an image that we're constructing in our heads.
E. This is an oddly hallucinogenic answer. "If you are on drugs, then the chair will have a rounder shape than normal". Normally, our psychological states don't affect the shape of objects.

Appendix: LR Questions By Type

Strengthen

Section I, #6
Section I, #12
Section III, #4
Section III, #8
Section III, #16 (exception)
Section III, #25

Weaken

Section I, #13
Section III, #21 (exception)

Sufficient Assumption

Section I, #1
Section III, #11
Section III, #14

Parallel Reasoning

Section I, #14
Section III, #24

Flawed Parallel Reasoning

Section I, #23
Section III, #15

Necessary Assumption

Section I, #16
Section I, #22
Section III, #19

Method of Reasoning

Section I, #2
Section I, #9

Must Be True

Section I, #17
Section III, #10

Most Strongly Supported

Section I, #8
Section I, #15
Section III, #17
Section III, #23

Paradox

Section I, #20
Section III, #3
Section III, #26

Principle

Section I, #19
Section I, #25
Section III, #6
Section III, #9
Section III, #13
Section III, #22

Identify The Conclusion

Section I, #5
Section I, #7
Section III, #12

Point At Issue

Section I, #10
Section III, #2

Role In Argument

Section I, #11

Complete The Argument

Section I, #4
Section III, #5

Flawed Reasoning

Section I, #3
Section I, #18
Section I, #21
Section I, #24
Section III, #1
Section III, #7
Section III, #18
Section III, #20

Thank You

First of all, thank you for buying this book. Writing these explanations has been the most satisfying work I have ever done. I sincerely hope they have been helpful to you, and I wish you success on the LSAT and as a lawyer.

If you left an Amazon review, you get an extra special thank you! I truly appreciate it. You're helping others discover Hacking The LSAT.

Thanks also to Anu Panil, who drew the diagrams for the logic games. Anu, thank you for making sense of the scribbles and scans I sent you. You are surely ready to master logic games after all the work you did.

Thanks to Alison Rayner, who helped me with the layout and designed the cover. If this book looks nice, she deserves credit. Alison caught many mistakes I would never have found by myself (any that remain are my own, of course).

Thanks to Ludovic Glorieux, who put up with me constantly asking him if a design change looked good or bad.

Finally, thanks to my parents, who remained broadly supportive despite me being crazy enough to leave law school to teach the LSAT. I love you guys.

About The Author

Graeme Blake lives in Montreal Canada. He first took the LSAT in June 2007, and scored a 177. It was love at first sight. He taught the LSAT for Testmasters for a couple of years before going to the University of Toronto for law school.

Upon discovering that law was not for him, Graeme began working as an independent LSAT tutor. He teaches LSAT courses in Montreal for Ivy Global and tutors students from all around the world using Skype.

He publishes a series of LSAT guides and explanations under the title Hacking The LSAT. Versions of these explanations can be found at LSAT Blog, Cambridge LSAT and Zen of 180, as well as amazon.com.

Graeme is also the moderator of www.reddit.com/r/LSAT, Reddit's LSAT forum. He worked for a time with 7Sage LSAT.

Graeme finds it unusual to write in the third person to describe himself, but he recognizes the importance of upholding publishing traditions. He wonders if many people read about the author pages.

You can find him at www.lsathacks.com and www.reddit.com/r/LSAT.

Graeme encourages you to get in touch by email, his address is graeme@lsathacks.com. Or you can call 514-612-1526. He's happy to hear feedback or give advice.

Further Reading

I hope you liked this book. If you did, I'd be very grateful if you took two minutes to review it on amazon. People judge a book by its reviews, and if you review this book you'll help other LSAT students discover it.

Ok, so you've written a review and want to know what to do next.

The most important LSAT books are the preptests themselves. Many students think they have to read every strategy guide under the sun, but you'll learn the most simply from doing real LSAT questions and analyzing your mistakes.

At the time of writing, there are 71 official LSATs. The most recent ones are best, but if you've got a while to study I recommend doing every test from 19 or from 29 onwards.

This series (Hacking The LSAT) is a bit different from other LSAT prep books. This book is not a strategy guide.

Instead, my goal is to let you do what my own students get to do when they take lessons with me: review their work with the help of an expert.

These explanations show you a better way to approach questions, and exactly why answers are right or wrong.

If you found this book useful, here's the list of other books in the series:

- Hacking The LSAT: Full Explanations For LSATs 29-38, Volume I
- Hacking The LSAT: Full Explanations For LSATs 29-38, Volume II
- LSAT 66 Explanations (Hacking The LSAT Series)
- LSAT 67 Explanations (Hacking The LSAT Series)
- LSAT 68 Explanations (Hacking The LSAT Series)
- LSAT 69 Explanations (Hacking The LSAT Series)
- LSAT 70 Explanations (Hacking The LSAT Series)

Keep an eye out, as I'll be steadily publishing explanations for earlier LSATs, starting with LSAT 65 and moving backwards.

If you *are* looking for strategy guides, try Manhattan LSAT or Powerscore. Unlike other companies, they use real LSAT questions in their books.

I've written a longer piece on LSAT books on Reddit. It includes links to the best LSAT books and preptests. If you're serious about the LSAT and want the best materials, I strongly recommend you read it:

http://redd.it/uf4uh

(this is a shortlink that takes you to the correct page)

Free LSAT Email Course

This book is just the beginning. It teaches you how to solve individual questions, but it's not designed to give you overall strategies for each section.

There's so much to learn about the LSAT. As a start, I've made a free, five day email course. Each day I'll send you an email teaching you what I know about a subject.

LSAT Email Course Overview

- Intro to the LSAT
- Logical Reasoning
- Logic Games
- Reading Comprehension
- How to study

What people say about the free LSAT course

These have been awesome. More please!!! - **Cailie**

Your emails are tremendously helpful. - **Matt**

Thanks for the tips! They were very helpful, and even make you feel like you studied a bit. Great insight and would love more! - **Haj**

Sign up for the free LSAT email course here:

http://lsathacks.com/email-course/

p.s. I've had people say this free email course is more useful than an entire Kaplan course they took. It's 100% free. Good luck - Graeme

Made in the USA
Lexington, KY
05 May 2014